DISCARD

OCT -- 1995

PRINCE GEORGE PUBLIC LIBRARY
887 DOMINION STREET
PRINCE GEORGE, B.C. V2L 5L1
563-9251

Our Tellings

Our Tellings is a collection of oral narratives gathered by a young Nlha7kápmx, Darwin Hanna, from the elders of his people. The tales have been passed from generation to generation, and they reveal how the Nlha7kápmx perceive their own history. By turns humorous, solemn, earthy, and sometimes harsh, these intriguingly detailed stories are designed to teach their listeners about nature, respect, and morality.

Our Tellings gathers together two types of narrative – sptákwelh and spílaxem. Sptákwelh, or creation stories, tell of a period in which the world was inhabited by animals in vaguely human form and with special powers. Coyote, Bear, Grizzly, and Owl were central figures. Some tellings in this group chronicle the acts of transformers, who travelled the countryside shaping and changing the existing order to resemble the world we know today. Spílaxem, or non-creation stories, tell of the history, way of life, and cultural teachings of the Nlha7kápmx people. These particular narratives were chosen because the elders thought that they were important to tell. They range from descriptions of the arrival of explorers and missionaries to reflections on the contemporary state of Nlha7kápmx culture.

The Nlha7kápmx, or Thompson, people are among the original inhabitants of the Fraser, Thompson, and Nicola river valleys in southwestern British Columbia. In *Our Tellings*, the Nlha7kápmx take charge of their own cultural revitalization. Many of the stories were told in the original Nlha7kápmx language and have been carefully translated to keep the voices of their tellers. Stories told in English have been set down more or less as they were told. Put together entirely by Nlha7kápmx people, *Our Tellings* articulates their culture in lasting form.

Darwin Hanna, a Nlha7kápmx and a Lytton Indian Band member, recently completed a law degree at the University of British Columbia.

Mamie Henry, a Nlha7kápmx elder and a Lytton Indian Band member, is a language and cultural studies instructor at Mestanta Technological Institute, Lytton, BC.

Compiled and edited by
Darwin Hanna and Mamie Henry

Our Tellings

Interior Salish Stories of the Nlha7kápmx People

UBC PRESS / VANCOUVER

PRINCE GEORGE PUBLIC LIBRARY

© In trust, Snk'y'peplxw (Coyote House) Language and Culture Society and Mamie Henry 1995

All rights reserved. No part of this publication may be reproduced, stored in a retrieval system, or transmitted, in any form or by any means, without prior written permission of the publisher.

Printed in Canada on acid-free paper ∞

ISBN 0-7748-0525-0

Canadian Cataloguing in Publication Data

Main entry under title:

Our tellings

ISBN 0-7748-0525-0

1. Ntlakyapamuk Indians – Folklore. 2. Indians of North America – British Columbia – Folklore. I. Hanna, Darwin, 1969- II. Henry, Mamie, 1922-
E99.N96097 1995 398.2'089'97907117 95-910169-1

This book has been published with the help of a grant from the Heritage Cultures and Languages Program, Multiculturalism and Citizenship Canada, Department of Canadian Heritage. UBC Press also gratefully acknowledges the ongoing support to its publishing program from the Canada Council, the Province of British Columbia Cultural Services Branch, and the Department of Communications of the Government of Canada.

All royalties will be used to purchase books for band schools.

UBC Press
University of British Columbia
6344 Memorial Road
Vancouver, BC V6T 1Z2
(604) 822-3259
Fax: 1-800-668-0821
E-mail: orders@ubcpress.ubc.ca

To the past that guides us into the future

Contents

Spílaxem (Non-Creation Stories)

Foreword

ONE DAY about four years ago the phone rang – it was Darwin Hanna. He told me he had just finished a research paper on the Nlha7kápmx traditional justice system for a criminology degree at Simon Fraser University, and he wondered if I might read it and comment on it. Shortly after the phone call we met and I listened as Darwin explained how he had combed the Fraser Canyon and Nicola Valley looking for people familiar with his research topic. With the assistance of his uncle, Nathan Spinks of Lytton, he had not only tracked down such persons but had tape-recorded many of his conversations with them. He was inspired by the elders and wanted to continue working with them.

Summer came and Darwin took a job with the Native-based Stein Valley Rediscovery Programme at Lytton. He assured me before his departure, however, that he would not forget his ethnographic project. Several months later he reappeared, this time with questions about funding agencies. He wanted to know more about them, where he could obtain application forms, and so on. I told him what I knew, and he returned a week or so later with the appropriate forms completed and oozing excitement at the prospect of spending the next eight months recording oral narratives in and around the Lytton area.

This series of back and forth calls and visits has characterized my relationship with Darwin Hanna. Over the years I have watched him tap into the rich bank of Nlha7kápmx traditional knowledge and grow to recognize both its power and its fragility. He has interacted with the elders in a spirit of respect and modesty, which I think accounts for much of his success, for they have responded openly to his polite and quiet enthusiasm. From the beginning of this recording project, Darwin has had a very close relationship with one particular elder – Mamie Henry of Lytton. For years, Mamie had listened with great interest to her own elders tell stories. She was one of the first to develop a writing system for the Nlha7kápmx language and also one of the first to teach it in the school system. She accompanied Darwin on many of his visits to various elders in order to facilitate introductions and, when necessary, to translate. She later translated into English many of the stories which they recorded. The result is this lovely volume, *Our Tellings: Interior Salish Stories of the Nlha7kápmx People*, a collection of traditional stories and teachings. It has been an honour to be on the periphery of its creation.

Although there are countless collections of British Columbia First Nations stories on the shelves today, few have been put together by First Nations tellers and translators themselves. James Teit, an anthropologist who worked out of his home in Spences Bridge around the turn of the century, undertook a similar project. Without the aid of a tape recorder, however, he had to rely on his memory. As a result, his records are mere sketches of the original tellings. He also had to submit his collections to the editorship of his mentor, Franz Boas. Because Boas was more interested in composite than in individual stories, he eliminated many of the names of the individual tellers and communities. On reading Teit's published collections today, one is left wondering exactly whose works and whose stories are being represented. Not so with *Our Tellings*, where, page by page, large numbers of people are named and acknowledged.

Unlike the pre-contact 'mythological' bias of most standard collections of North American First Nations stories, *Our Tellings* includes everything from Nlha7kápmx accounts of first explorers, settlers, and missionaries to contemporary reflections on Nlha7kápmx life. One highlight is a long discussion between Darwin and his grandparents, Bea and Fred Hanna, on topics ranging from doctoring to basket-making.

Another special feature of *Our Tellings* is its authenticity. Translations of stories told originally in the Nlha7kápmx language are the work of local translators such as Marion Bent, Mamie Henry, Dorothy Ursaki, and Bert Seymour. This being the case, the stories retain much of their original colour and detail. Mildred Michell's incorporation of dialogue in her telling of the well-known story 'Ntl'ík'semtm (Coyote's Son)' provides a good example of this.

> Blue Grouse felt around for his food, then Fool Hen felt around for her food and said, 'Well! Where is it?'
> Blue Grouse said, 'You took it!'
> 'No!' said Fool Hen.
> 'But there was a hand there!' said Blue Grouse.
> 'No! I didn't take it!' said Fool Hen.

The stories that were related in English appear as told. Unlike the vague and awkward translations and summaries characteristic of many older collections, those represented here are colourful and precise. Herb Manuel's characterization of Coyote, in 'Coyote and Wolf,' is typical:

> Coyote was a show-off. He was kind of always undernourished. He was, in human flesh, a skinny, tall man with drawn-in cheeks, and when he spoke, he spoke with a drawn-in voice. He spoke funny. You knew it was him when you heard his voice. He spoke this way. There was no way he could get away from his speech.

References to 'respect' and 'humility' appear everywhere throughout this volume. In 'Sore Man,' Mabel Joe states she is somewhat unsure of what she is telling: 'I don't know if this is the correct story of the Sore Man. Anyway, it's pretty close.' Others explicitly acknowledge the persons from whom they learned their stories: 'I am going to tell stories that my grandfather told me.'

Because this collection is the creation of Nlha7kápmx themselves, it includes countless little-known details about the local area. For example, in 'Coyote and Wolf,' Herb Manuel tells Darwin how Coyote's house, a low-lying mountain, was once a prime feature of the town of Merritt:

> Right at the King Garden Manor there was a low-lying mountain – a little hill. I've seen it. It's called Senk'iy̓apáplhxw – Coyote's House. That house was pure gravel, and they used it to pave the road from Merritt, up the Nicola, to Sulús, and up towards Princeton Road – as far as they could while the gravel lasted. It was pea gravel. The hill was beautiful ... That was his house. The town of Merritt, or the government, or the highways, or whatever levelled it. That was where he lived.

Similarly, Bill Walkem of Spences Bridge speaks of a tree that appears, to the unknowing viewer, to be nothing out of the ordinary. But to those familiar with its history, it is a 'dancing tree':

> I would figure [it's] about five hundred years old, more or less. It's a master. It stands, the sun shines on it and makes it feel lonely for the Spirit ... When people, that is, those that have gone, wanted to praise nature and the sun, they picked the most beautiful tree in the valley, and through that tree, hope carried on for another couple of hundred years. I guess that tree was born before Columbus.

This special collection celebrates community, nature, and, especially, the age-old oral tradition of the Nlha7kápmx of south central British Columbia. Like Bill Walkem's dancing tree, it is a treasure.

Wendy Wickwire, Head
Ts''kel Programme for First Nations
Graduate Students, UBC

Acknowledgments

I WOULD LIKE TO THANK Mamie Henry for accompanying me on many miles of road looking for sptákwelh (creation stories) and for translating many of them. Her knowledge of our language and culture have been invaluable, and her keen interest in preserving them has had a great impact on me – because of Mamie's encouragement, I am now learning Nlha7kapmxtsín (the Nlha7kápmx language). I am deeply grateful to her.

I would like to thank Chief David Walkem, Councillor M. Rose Spence, Councillor Jean York, and the membership of the Cook's Ferry Band for providing the necessary funding to get this project completed during the summer of 1993. I would also like to thank Leslie Tepper of the Canadian Museum of Civilization for securing funding for the summer of 1993 and the Canada Council Explorations Programme for providing funding for the period between January and August 1992. For the final stages of drafting the manuscript I received an Aboriginal Arts Development Award (Cultural Services Branch, BC Ministry of Small Business, Tourism and Culture).

The Nlaka'pamux Nation Tribal Council provided technical support; in particular, between January and August 1992, the use of its computer, photocopier, and tape recorder. I especially thank it for purchasing a professional tape recorder for my use – without it, my work would have been extremely difficult. I would also like to especially thank the late Eric Phillips for helping me in my research, particularly with computer problems. He was always there for me, and he showed me how to gather information from the elders.

I thank the staff of the Nicola Valley Tribal Council for referring me to some of the elders in the Nicola Valley.

Chief Byron Spinks of the Lytton First Nation and Lytton Elementary School principal Jean York encouraged me and assisted me in acquiring funds for this project.

I am greatly indebted to Dr Wendy Wickwire. Without her keen interest in our culture, I do not think this project would have taken place. Wendy also supported my funding applications and has continued to support this project. Her enthusiasm rubbed off on me.

Dorothy Ursaki was invaluable to me, as she both translated stories and taught me about our language. Her unending sense of humour and connection to all the goings-on within our nation made my visits with her full of fun. My aunt, Marion Bent, also translated many stories and taught me about our ways. I thank them both very much. Bert and Joyce Seymour and Jimmy Toodlican accompanied me on two interviews and helped translate stories. Jack Joe also accompanied me on several interviews. I would especially like to thank my great-uncle, Nathan Spinks, for taking time to explain how things are done. His keen interest in the project and the many stories he shared with me kept me interested in, and focused on, this project.

My cousins, Cathy Howett and Don Johnson, installed Nlha7kápmx linguistic fonts for Wordperfect on my computer and provided advice on linguistics.

Doug Sanderson, a Cree originally from The Pas, Manitoba, and now residing in Vancouver, took photographs of elders and of Nlha7kápmx country.

I would like to thank Randy Bouchard and Dorothy Kennedy for generously allowing me to use stories that they and Mamie Henry collected between 1968 and 1973 and for editing those stories for the current collection. Kennedy and Bouchard both provided information about some of the place-names that appear in this text, some photographs, the orthographic key for the Nlha7kápmx alphabet, and background materials on Nlha7kápmx ethnography, mythology, and linguistics. Randy Bouchard kindly checked the final Nlha7kápmx transcriptions. His work in promoting Native languages over the past twenty-five years has included devising a practical writing system for Nlha7kapmxtsín. He and Dorothy Kennedy work with the BC Indian Language Project, a non-profit society dedicated to the documentation of the province's aboriginal languages and cultures.

Most important, I would like to thank all of the elders who welcomed me into their homes and shared with me their knowledge. They are: the late Louie Phillips, the late Hilda Austin, Mildred Michell, Susannah Phillips, Mabel Joe, Edna Malloway, Bert and Joyce Seymour, Norman Dunstan, Ada and Peter Bob, Herb Manuel, Willard Angus, Phil and Annie Acar, Tom George, Paul Oppenheim, Rose Tait, Rosie Joe, Ethel Isaac, Margaret and the late Smitty Bent, the late Stella Snow, Mandy Brown, Edna Kane, John and Hilda Isaac, Percy Minnaberriet, Bill Walkem, and the late Annie York.

In the three years I have spent researching this book throughout Nlha7kápmx territory, people too numerous to mention have generously offered assistance and encouragement. I thank them all – especially my fellow Nlha7kápmx students at UBC.

In closing, a special thanks to my family members, especially my grandparents, for their encouragement. And I would like to thank my núx̱wa7 (sweetheart) Cynthia, and her daughter Lauren, for listening to all of the stories and providing me with support and encouragement.

Our Tellings

Introduction

THIS BOOK is a collection of Nlha7kápmx stories which Mamie Henry and I have gathered from our elders in order to help carry on, and to share with others, the storytelling traditions of our people. 'Nlha7kápmx' can be translated as people or nation, and it denotes a distinct cultural and linguistic group in southwest British Columbia.

Yesterday

According to James Teit, a Scottish ethnographer who lived and worked in K'k̲émtsin (Spences Bridge) in the early twentieth century, '"Nlha7káp" [means] "reach the bottom or base," with reference to passing or [going] through a narrow place to the bottom or base, as [in] a canyon, for instance, [and] the suffix "mx" [means] "people."' This name, wrote Teit, 'was applied to Lytton and the people there in a general sense and [was] extended to embrace the whole tribe or people speaking the Thompson language.'[1] 'Nlaka'pamux' is a common spelling, but, unlike 'Nlha7kápmx,' it is not linguistically accurate. We were also known as the 'Thompson' (the Thompson River runs through our territory), the 'Pipe Stem,' the 'Couteaux,' and the 'Knife' Indians.

Our people live along the Fraser River Canyon between Spuzzum and Tl'k̲émtsin (Lytton; specifically, the village of Lytton at the confluence of the Fraser and Thompson rivers); from Tl'k̲émtsin

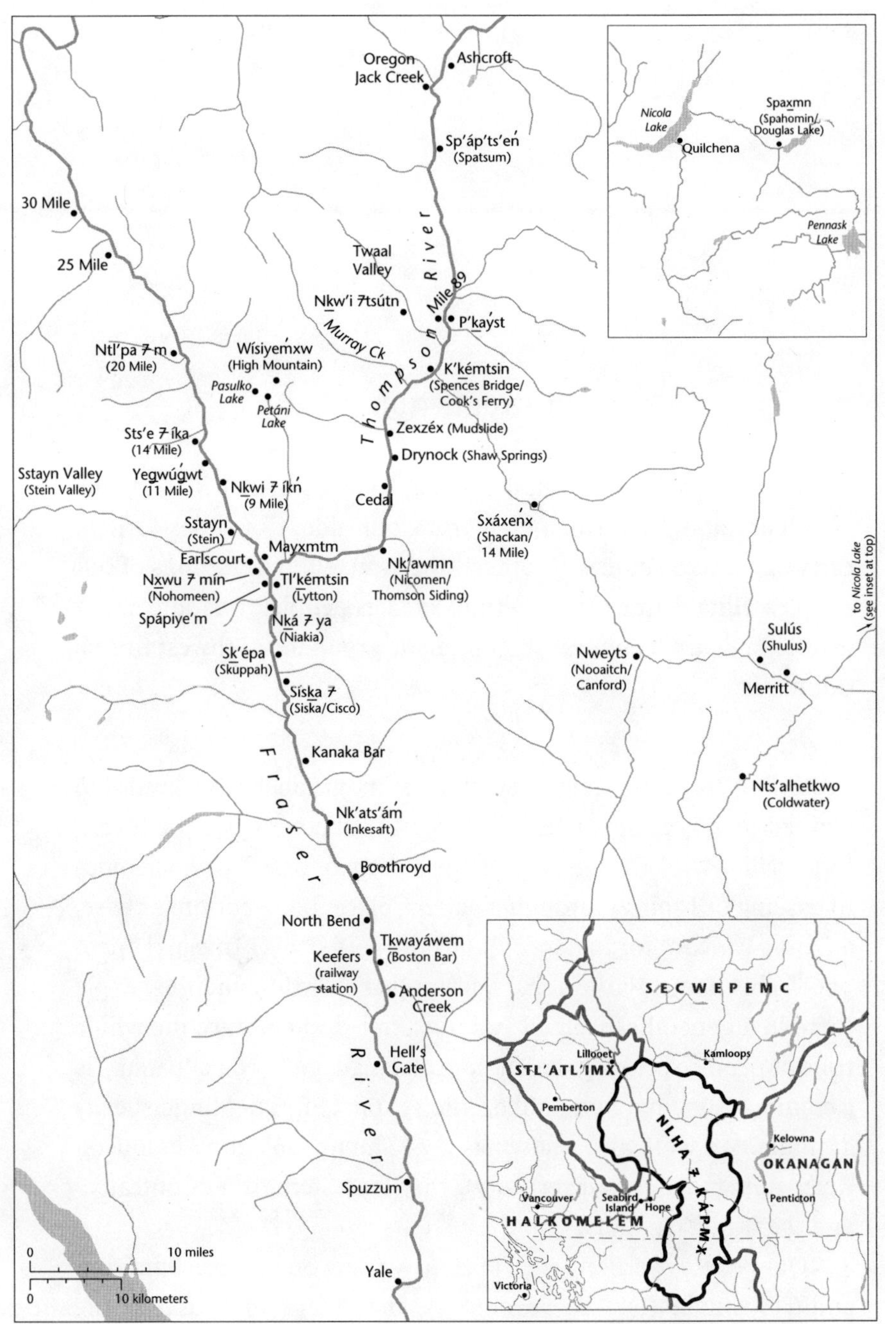

NLHA7KÁPMX TERRITORY

thirty miles north to Texas Creek (just south of Lillooet); along the Thompson River between Tl'k̲émtsin and Ashcroft; along the Nicola River from K'k̲émtsin to Quilchena; and in the Coldwater Valley. Nlha7kápmx head chief Sexpínlhemx (also known as David Spintlum, 1812-87) defined the 'posts' or boundaries of our country:

> One post up the Fraser at [Fountain] – one down the Fraser at Spuzzum – one up the Thompson River at Ashcroft – one up the Nicola River at Quilchena – one down the Similkameen River at Tcutcuwī xa [near Hedley]. All the country between these posts is my country and the lands of my people. At Lytton is my centre-post. It is the middle of my house, and I sit there. All the country to the headwaters of all the streams running into the valleys between these posts is also my territory in which my children gather food. We extend to meet the boundaries of the hunting territories of other tribes. All around over this country I have spoken of, I have jurisdiction. I know no white man's boundaries or posts. If the whites have put up posts and divided up my country, I do not recognize them. They have not consulted me. They have broken my house without my consent. All Indian tribes have the same as posts and recognized boundaries, and the chiefs know them since long before the first whites came to the country.[2]

Linguistically, we form part of the Interior Salish division of the Salishan language family. Interior Salish can be further divided into northern and southern subgroups. The northern subgroup, to which our language belongs, comprises the Stl'atl'imx (Lillooet) and Secwepemc (Shuswap) languages; the southern subgroup comprises the Columbian, Okanagan, Kalispel, and Coeur d'Alene languages.[3] Even though we are culturally and linguistically very similar to the peoples belonging to these groups, we are a distinct nation. Many people assume that our culture was less elaborate than that of coastal groups and less romantic than that of prairie groups, but this is not so.

We were a semi-nomadic people, and our economy was based

on fishing, hunting, gathering, and trading. In the fall and winter we lived in s7istkn (pithouses), and in the spring and summer we lived in tipis covered with bulrush mats. We had a distinct belief system and social organization.

Although it is not possible to determine what our population base was during pre-contact times, historical accounts and records indicate that it was well over 5,000.[4] The first European account of our population size is found in the journals of Simon Fraser. When he came upon Tl'k̲émtsin at the confluence of the Thompson and Fraser rivers in June 1808, he stated that '[the Nlha7kápmx] people were sitting in rows, to the number of twelve hundred; and I had to shake hands with all of them.'[5] And according to Indian Reserve Commissioner Gilbert Sproat, 'On 17 July 1879, seventy-one years after Simon Fraser, there was another gathering of 1,200 at Lytton.'[6] Finally, just before 1900, our elders told Teit:

> The old people say that forty or fifty years ago, when travelling along Thompson River, the smoke of Indian camp-fires was always in view. This will be better understood when it is noted that the course of Thompson River is very tortuous, and that in many places one can see but a very short distance up or down the river. The old Indians compare the number of people formerly living in the vicinity of Lytton to 'ants about an ant-hill.'[7]

According to Teit, there were seventy Nlha7kápmx villages,[8] varying considerably in size. He estimated that the villages at Spuzzum and North Bend were the largest.[9] 'Many of the villages ... are very small, consisting of two or three families; while others are large, and contain about a hundred or more inhabitants.'[10] Our population plummeted in the late 1800s and the early 1900s due to smallpox and tuberculosis; this, of course, was disastrous.

Today

Today, there are approximately 5,000 Nlha7kápmx. Although many of us still reside in the same communities as did our ancestors, many of us also live outside our territory. Currently, elected chiefs and band councils administer both Department of Indian Affairs and Northern Development (DIAND) programs and self-governance programs. Under the Indian Act, the Nlha7kápmx Nation comprises sixteen bands. Our people still rely heavily on such natural resources as salmon, plant foods, and wild game; and in the last few decades our language and traditions have been revitalized through gatherings, cultural and language infusion programs in both public and band schools, band initiatives, and the teachings of our elders.

Personal History

I grew up having two backgrounds: my mother, Lynn Murtland, is French and Irish; my late father, Herb Hanna, was Nlha7kápmx and a member of the Lytton Indian Band. My parents separated when I was a baby, and I was raised by my mother (who has no close relatives). We lived in Richmond until I was six, and then we moved to Maple Ridge, where I finished my schooling. When I was young I had a vague idea that I was Indian. When I was in kindergarten the teacher told the whole class that another student and I were Indian because our skin was dark. When I was seven or eight, I met, for the first time, my paternal grandparents. I stayed with them over the Easter holidays, and I can still remember some of what I learned at that time. When I was growing up people would always try to guess what my background was – Mexican, East Indian, Hawaiian, Spanish, Italian – but they never guessed that I was 'Indian.' Sometimes I was called derogatory names, and often I had to endure hearing stories that disparaged Indians. I suppose that the people who told these stories either didn't know I was Indian or just assumed that, as I had been raised in a non-Native environment, I would agree with them.

I first visited Tl'k̲émtsin when I was about ten years old, when my family had a reunion at Pasulko Lake in the Petáni (Botanie) Valley. There, I met more of my paternal relatives. I remember playing the bone game and bringing home salmon that my uncle had netted. This trip instilled in me a real desire to understand my Nlha7kápmx roots. After this trip, I went to the library and discovered that I was a 'Thompson Indian.' This puzzled me. I couldn't understand why we were called Thompson Indians when my relatives lived on the Fraser River at Nk̲á7ya (Niakia – a settlement one mile south of Tl'k̲émtsin on the west side of the Fraser River). When I was in Grade 7, I applied for and received my Indian status card, which declared that I was a member of the Lytton Indian Band. (At that time I was not aware that many of my relatives were denied their status because, under the Indian Act, Indian women who married non-Indian men lost their status, as did their children. And, continuing in typical sexist form, under this same act, non-Indian women who married Indian men were given full Indian status.)

When I was in my early teens I went with my dad and grandparents to a wedding in Terrace, and, at the invitation of my relatives (five of my father's first cousins married Tsimshian whom they had met at St George's Indian Residential School), I spent part of the summer in Kitsumkalum, a Tsimshian community three miles to the west of Terrace. During my numerous other stays in this community, I learned more about First Nations culture. However, it was from my paternal grandparents, who lived near my home in Maple Ridge and with whom I frequently visited, that I learned most about my culture and history. My grandparents were raised in the Tl'k̲émtsin area (the heart of Nlha7kápmx country), where they lived the old way. In 1974, they retired and moved to Langley, and I spent many hours listening to them and learning from them. I also learned a lot from the many relatives and friends who often visited them.

After graduating from high school I made more visits to Tl'k̲émtsin. During college and university, I took classes in First Nations culture and history, and I started to ask my grandparents more questions. I was going through a cultural awakening. During this time many First Nations issues had surfaced, especially those specific to fishing rights and land claims. First Nations protests were being held over proposed logging on Lyell Island (Haida), Meares Island (Nuu-Chah-Nulth), and in the Stein Valley (Stl'átl'imx and Nlha7kápmx). Then there was the Oka crisis, which united many First Nations peoples. For my part, I registered in a Tl'k̲émtsin-based cultural program called Stein Rediscovery. I spent two weeks in the Stein Valley, where I was actively introduced to spirituality, the sweat lodge, drumming and singing, plant use, and many other aspects of our culture.

People such as myself, who have attended Anglo-Saxon schools and learned about Anglo-Saxon culture, have been assimilated into mainstream Canadian society. Because we have never been allowed to become intimate with our own cultures, we are now actively searching for and recovering them. Of course, cultural revitalization creates confusion and uneasiness. Some First Nations people, myself included, are always pondering the relationship between living in the modern world and attending cultural gatherings, practising First Nations spirituality, and exercising aboriginal hunting, fishing, and gathering rights.

In my final year of criminology at Simon Fraser University (SFU), I was given the opportunity to do fieldwork. I chose to go to Tl'k̲émtsin and work with the Nlaka'pamux Nation Tribal Council; I immersed myself in meeting new people and becoming involved with community events. I was asked to research and prepare a paper on the Nlha7kápmx justice system, and, in so doing, I had a wonderful time travelling to our different communities with my great-uncle, Nathan Spinks. Together, Nathan and I taped, translated, talked, and reminisced with many elders. My final paper, 'Justice the Nlha7kápmx Way,' was well received not only by my course instructor but also by our people. Furthermore, I learned so much about our language and culture that I decided to do more of this kind of work. However, I had to return to Maple Ridge to finish my degree at SFU.

I was determined to do more field recording, and so, with the help of Wendy Wickwire, I applied for a Canada Council Explorations

Grant. After completing my degree, I was awarded this grant, and, for the next eight months, I worked on recording the oral narratives of my people. As this project was so heartily supported by many of my people, I decided to turn my collection into a book. I did this because I believe that it is essential that our oral traditions be readily available to everyone in our communities.

I have been actively trying to learn my language and history, but it has been difficult, for many are not yet ready for cultural revitalization. This may be traced to the devastating effects of colonialism: the fur trade, the gold rush of 1858, disease, missionaries, the construction of the Canadian National Railways (CNR) and the Canadian Pacific Railway (CPR), the Indian Act, the residential school system, the Hell's Gate slide of 1913 (which temporarily destroyed the salmon fishery), alcohol, and drugs have all taken, and many continue to take, their toll. St George's Indian Residential School (1901-77), attended by both my father and my paternal grandparents, was one of the products of the federal government's policy of assimilation. I have heard countless stories about how the students at St George's were beaten for attempting to speak their own languages. As a result of this kind of treatment, some two or more generations of Nlha7kápmx are afraid to speak our language, and many people of my generation can speak only English. Since 1973, however, largely thanks to Mamie Henry, the Nlha7kápmx language has been taught in the schools at Lytton.

Non-Stop Collecting

It is important to realize that, since White contact, many people have been collecting stories from our area. Hundreds of stories have been told to researchers, and most of them are not available to our own people. James Teit, who was fluent in Nlha7kapmxtsín, did ethnographic work among our people from 1894 to 1922. He published several volumes and papers on 271 creation stories as well as on general ethnography. Franz Boas, who edited most of Teit's work, visited Tl'k̲émtsin for three days in July 1888 and collected five stories, which were published in German.[11] In 1899, Charles Hill-Tout published ten stories which were told to him by Chief Mischelle of Tl'k̲émtsin; in 1898, Marion Smith collected stories from the lower Fraser Canyon region and presented them in a thesis; in the 1940s, Noel Stewart, a teacher at St George's Indian Resi-dential School, published ten Coyote stories; and, from 1981 to 1983, Steve Egesdahl collected thirty stories from elders in Tl'k̲émtsin.

Indeed, beginning in approximately 1897, our elders were regularly tape-recorded by anthropologists, ethnographers, linguists, archaeologists, ethnobotanists, and so on.[12] Some of the elders who told me stories had been tape-recorded dozens of times, evidence of the work being done over many years to promote cultural and linguistic retention among Native peoples. *Our Tellings* not only attempts to carry on this work but more specifically represents an effort by the Nlha7kápmx people to take charge of our own cultural revitalization.

The Stories

Many elders recall, when they were children, being told stories at night (these stories, told repeatedly, taught them about nature, respect, morality, and proper behaviour; they also served as a form of entertainment). The elders also recall hearing stories at gatherings, funerals, potlatches, hunting and fishing camps, root- and berry-gathering camps, and so on – but many have forgotten them. According to Mildred Michell, 'When my dad died he must've took the stories with him.' Mamie Henry feels that elders have forgotten stories because they have nobody to tell them to, their grandchildren being too busy playing sports or watching television to listen. When asked if they knew any stories, some elders replied that they did not, as they were never around *their* elders. Some reflected that they only remembered the dirty parts, but they did not elaborate. One elder jokingly stated, 'Ask by the graveyard,' for when the elders die, they take with them an encyclopedia of knowledge.

At the many gatherings, funerals, and meetings I attended after

I returned to Nlha7kápmx territory, I did not hear many stories about Coyote or any of the other animals. What I did hear was usually about Coyote's character or perhaps a fragment of a longer story. I don't know when the stories stopped being told on a regular basis, but I think it was quite recently. This is not to suggest that people don't tell stories any more; it is just that fewer people are telling them at fewer places. However, there are people, not yet elders, who are now learning the art of storytelling. Today, the most prevalent stories are probably those which deal with family relations.

Over the course of two years, I recorded many stories, most of them being 'sptákwelh' or creation stories, which tell of events that occurred when the world was populated by animals in human form; others being 'spílax̱em' or non-creation stories, which tell of events that occurred during historical time. Mamie would often say that these recordings were treasures.

The Tellers

In order to discuss our stories with an elder, it is necessary to have a basic understanding of our traditions. I heard short tales about Coyote, Grizzly, and the Bear brothers from my grandparents, but I needed more information. So I began reading the stories that Teit had collected at the beginning of the twentieth century. From these I gained a basic understanding of our stories. I also talked to my great-uncle Nathan, who sat me down and told me to ask the elders about Ntl'ík'semtm (Coyote's son). He said, 'If you ask about that one story, the rest will follow naturally.' So on our first visit with Mildred Michell, Mamie Henry and I asked about that story. Mildred responded, and it is with this hour-long story that *Our Tellings* begins.

I was fortunate to be assisted by Mamie Henry, an elder of the Lytton Indian Band dedicated to teaching our language and culture to younger generations. She tells her own story:

> I was born and raised in Anderson Creek [just south of Boston Bar], where my dad was also born and raised. My mother was from 11 Mile, Lytton. I didn't go to school until I was nine years

old because I didn't want to go away from my family. When my younger brother became old enough to go to school I agreed to go. We attended St George's Indian Residential School. In 1940, I married George Henry of Lytton. There I raised my four children – Fred, Vivian, Pauline, and Joseph.

In 1968 I met Randy Bouchard, and he got me interested in working with him on our language. I translated Nlha7kápmx legends for him. In 1971 he introduced me to Tammy Hurst, a UBC student. We gathered more stories. It was not very easy in those early years to get stories from the elders. They seemed embarrassed to tell their stories. I started to learn how to read and write the Nlha7kápmx language. It was a lot of hard work. I asked Randy, my teacher, 'Why am I doing this?' Randy said, 'Oh, someday you will teach your people.'

Around 1973 we had completed some language lessons and a dictionary, and I started to teach Nlha7kapmxtsín [the Nlha7kápmx language] and Nlha7kápmx studies at Kumsheen Secondary School in Lytton. In 1982 I taught preschool through to Grade 7 at Lytton Elementary. In 1986 I retired from teaching.

When I think back a few years, it was difficult teaching language to the students because it was something new to them. Our language was in trouble. In 1993 I started teaching again at Mestanta Technological Institute in Lytton, a Lytton First Nations school. I am enjoying it all over again. Students are eager to learn their language – a big difference from 1973.

I helped Darwin collect legends and stories. We visited everyone whom we thought would have a story to tell – from Spuzzum to Douglas Lake to Coldwater. People were proud to tell their stories, even though they couldn't remember everything. Some of the stories were family histories. Some told their stories in Nlha7kápmx. It was easier than in 1971, when people were shy. One person who forgot her stories blamed it on the fact that she didn't have any grandchildren to tell them to, and she also blamed St George's Indian Residential School.

Mamie and I travelled throughout our territory, and she introduced me to many tellers. We travelled from Tl'k̲émtsin to 25 Mile on the westside road towards Lillooet; to Sísk̲a7 (Siska), Boothroyd, Tk̲wayáwem (Boston Bar), North Bend, Spuzzum, and as far as Yale; and to Nk̲'awmn (Nicomen), K'k̲émtsin (Spences Bridge), Cache Creek, Sxáxeňx (Shackan), Sulús (Shulus), Nts'alhetkwo (Coldwater), and Spax̲mn (Douglas Lake). We covered every corner of the Nlha7kápmx nation looking for tellers. I also visited some elders alone and some with Jack Joe of Sulús and Bert and Joyce Seymour. When I visited an elder I would say, 'I am Fred and Bea Hanna's imts [grandson]' or 'Tselhnéga n skwast [My name is Tselhnéga].' Right away they would know who I was and where I was from. Tselhnéga is my great-grandfather's Nlha7kápmx name, and it was given to me by my grandparents in the spring of 1992. My great-grandfather's English name was John Hanna, and he was from Kanaka Bar (during the gold rush of 1858, many Hawaiians settled at Kanaka Bar and intermarried with Nlha7kápmx; the name Hanna is of Hawaiian origin). He was well known throughout our territory, for he hired our people to pick hops in Chilliwack. My grandfather, Fred Hanna, is also known as Tselhnéga. Upon hearing this name, people then would tell me how they were related to me or how they knew my grandparents. My other great-grandfather, Harry Sam, was also quite well known and was the chief of Nk̲á7ya (Niakia).

Many elders provided stories; however, there were some who did not want to be tape-recorded. For example, when Mamie was collecting stories in the 1970s, one elder from K'k̲émtsin wouldn't be taped because she believed that it would take her voice away; she also told Mamie that she wouldn't let her niece take her picture because she believed it would take her shadow away. If you are not a relative or friend, elders are not likely to share their stories with you. Furthermore, some stories are not meant to be shared publicly, as they are either valued family possessions or they contain information of a sensitive nature (e.g., stories about wrongdoings).

The Translations/Transcriptions

Stories told in English were transcribed by me and have undergone very little editing. Stories told in Nlha7kápmx were translated by Mamie Henry, Dorothy Ursaki, Bert Seymour, and/or Marion Bent (a Native Studies teacher in Tl'k̲émtsin) – all of whom have been Nlha7kapmxtsín consultants for years. Bert's and Marion's translations were used to check Mamie's and Dorothy's translations, and so most of them do not appear in this collection. Mamie Henry preferred to translate the stories by herself, listening to the tape line by line, then writing down what she heard. Dorothy Ursaki had me play the tape, then signalled me to stop, at which point she wrote while I rewound the tape in order to repeat the process. With Bert Seymour, Marion Bent, and Bea Hanna, I played the tape and waited for them to signal me to stop, at which point I recorded their translations.

The reader will notice a marked difference between the stories that have been translated from Nlha7kápmx and those that have been transcribed in English – the former being polished and flowing smoothly, the latter being rough and having a stop-and-start quality to them. For the most part, this merely reflects the difference between how one sounds when speaking one's first language and how one sounds when speaking a language with which one is not completely comfortable. Although intrusive editing could have made those stories that were transcribed verbatim sound much like those that were translated from Nlha7kápmx, I have decided not to do this, as it would have meant sacrificing both the immediacy of their tellings and the personalities of their tellers.

Clearly, transforming the oral into the written word results in some loss of meaning. Aside from the difficulty of translating certain Nlha7kápmx words and phrases into English, the reader cannot see the hand gestures, body movements, and settings that are a part of oral recitations. The reader also cannot hear voice inflections or know what discussion took place before, during, and after the story was told. Often tellers told me to turn off the tape; in other words, they had control over what would and what would not appear in this book. Because I always tried to be sensitive to the elders' desires, I did not always record everything they said.

While I was doing my recording, I contacted researchers whom I knew had collected stories among our elders in previous years. Randy Bouchard and Dorothy Kennedy of the British Columbia Indian Language Project responded and generously allowed me to add stories that they, Tammy Hurst, and Mamie Henry had collected between 1968 and 1973 from Walter Isaac, Rosie Skuki, Christine Bobb, Mary Williams, Anthony Joe, and Annie York. All these stories were translated by Mamie Henry and were transcribed by the British Columbia Indian Language Project. I also obtained some stories collected by CBC journalist Imbert Orchard in 1965, as told in English by Annie York of Spuzzum.[13] I transcribed these and, with very minor editing, included them in this collection.

ONE DAY I was sitting with Bert and Joyce Seymour at their home in Sxáxeńx. Jimmy Toodlican, a neighbour, was there too. Together, Bert and Jimmy were translating stories. At the end, Bert thanked me for sharing some of the stories I had heard. This is what *Our Tellings* is all about – the sharing of stories. Many of our parents and grandparents listened to these stories every night until people stopped saying 'yi7áy' ('yes' said as encouragement to a storyteller). Members of the present generation, many of whom have been cut off from their elders, have not had the opportunity to learn about their backgrounds and to become familiar with these stories. Thus, it is important to print them. I hope, upon reading this book, that Nlha7kápmx readers will seek stories from their own parents, grandparents, relatives, and friends and so continue transmitting our cultural knowledge. And I hope that non-Nlha7kápmx readers will learn something about our culture and history.

NOTES

1 James Teit, Unpublished ethnographic and linguistic fieldnotes, American Philosophical Library, Philadelphia (also in BC Archives and Records Service, Victoria, microfilm reels A236-A268).

2 Ibid.

3 Laurence C. Thompson, 'Salishan and the Northwest,' in Lyle Campbell and Marianne Mithun, eds., *The Languages of Native America*, 692-765 (Austin, TX: University of Texas Press).

4 James Teit, 'The Thompson Indians of British Columbia,' *Memoirs of the American Museum of Natural History* 2 (1900):163-392. See also p. 175, where it is estimated that our pre-contact population was at least 5,000.

5 W. Kaye Lamb, *The Letters and Journals of Simon Fraser, 1806-1808* (Toronto: Macmillan 1960), 87.

6 Public Archives of Canada, G.M. Sproat to Superintendent General of Indian Affairs, Lytton, 26 July 1879, Black series, RG10, vol. 3696, file 15,316.

7 Teit, 'Thompson Indians of British Columbia,' 175, note 4.

8 Ibid., 169, 171-4.

9 Ibid., 170.

10 Ibid., 174.

11 Franz Boas, *Indianische Sagen von der Nord-Pacifischen Kuste Amerikas* (Berlin: Verlag von A.Asher), prepared for the BC Indian Language Project as 'Indian Myths and Legends from the North Pacific Coast of America,' Dietrich Bertz, trans. (1977), Randy Bouchard and Dorothy Kennedy, eds. (1980-1).

12 These people include Nancy Turner, Andrea Laforet, Jan-Marie Martell, Wendy Wickwire, Gordon Mohs, Richard Daly, Dave Wyatt, Helen Bromley, Leslie Tepper, and Paul Kroeber. It is interesting to note that, beginning in 1897)., James Teit made wax-cylinder recordings of Nlha7kápmx songs and speeches.

13 It should be noted that Laurence and Terry Thompson worked with Annie York for over twenty years compiling a Nlha7kápmx dictionary. They collected many stories from her and other elders throughout our territory.

Sptákwelh (Creation Stories)

Sptákwelh (Creation Stories)

WHEN MAMIE AND I VISITED ELDERS, we would ask them if they knew any sptákwelh. In the sptákwelh period, the world was inhabited by animals in vaguely human form. Central figures were Coyote, Bear, Grizzly, Chipmunk, Owl, and Crow. These stories are commonly referred to as 'legends,' 'myths,' 'fairy-tales,' 'transformer stories,' 'folklore,' and 'fables.' However, as the events recounted in sptákwelh are believed to have really occurred, I refer to them as creation stories.

James Teit collected many sptákwelh, which he compiled in several volumes, and in *Traditions of the Thompson River Indians of British Columbia* he analyses them as follows:

> At one time, very long ago, the earth was very different from what it is at present. There were no trees, and many kinds of bushes and plants were wanting; neither was there any salmon or other fish, nor any berries. The people who lived during this age were called spêtā'kl. They were mostly animals, who, nevertheless, had human form. They were gifted in magic; and their children used to reach maturity in a few months. There were among them cannibals, and many mysterious persons.
>
> After a time certain men successively appeared on the earth, travelling here and there, working wonders, changing and modifying the existing order of things. Gradually many of the spêtā'kl who were bad were shorn of their powers, driven out of the country, or were transformed into birds, fishes, animals and trees. The greatest of these transformers was the Old Coyote who, it is said, was sent by the Old Man to put the world in order, so that the people might live more easily and happily. At the same time three brothers called Qoā'qLqaL travelled all over the country, working miracles. At that period there lived still another transformer. His name was Kokwē'la. The brothers were finally transformed into stone, while the Old Coyote, after having finished his work, disappeared. Then

> the Old Man travelled over the country. He saw that there were still many bad people on the earth; therefore he gathered all the people together, and began to separate the good from the bad. Having done this, he transformed all the evil ones into birds and animals, cursing them and assigning them to the different spheres which they were henceforth to occupy, while the good people he led forth over the country, settling them in different places.
>
> Thus ended the age of the spêtā'kl, and since then the earth and its inhabitants have been much the same as they are at present. All the animals, birds, and fishes were originally people, whilst the Indians of the present day are the descendants of the good people who were left on the earth by the Old Man.
>
> These events are told at length in the legends of the Coyote, Qoā'qLqaL, Kokwē'la, and the Old Man (pp.19-20).

The Coyote stories are the most well-known sptákwelh, followed closely by those about Grizzly and the Bear Cubs/Transformers and those about Owl. During my visits to my grandparents, my grandfather would occasionally talk about Coyote. Mostly we would talk about his character – how sly he was. The elders would often tell me how bad he was (e.g., Coyote often engaged in inappropriate sexual behaviour). The longest and most well-known of the Coyote stories is 'Ntl'ík'semtm.' Some of these stories contain remnants of the Coyote language, and both Louie Phillips and Herb Manuel would talk or sing like Coyote in certain parts of their tellings.

The stories about Grizzly and the Bear Cubs and Transformers tell of four bear cubs (the Transformers) who escaped from the wrath of Grizzly. The youngest cub was named Sk̲wik̲wtl'k̲wetl't, and he was supposed to be the most powerful. It was Sk̲wik̲wtl'k̲wetl't who often gave things their present form.

Many elders still recall that, because of stories about Owl, they were scared to go out in the dark when they were children. They were told that Owl would get them. My grandmother once told me that when she finally ventured out when it was dark she was scared of the moon because she didn't know what it was.

Ntl'ík'semtm (Coyote's Son)

Told by Mildred Michell
Translated by Mamie Henry

THIS LEGEND is about Ntl'ík'semtm. There once lived a Coyote whose son had two wives. Coyote said to himself, 'I'll fix things with my son and I will take his wives.' One of his daughters-in-law had a boy. Coyote went outside of the pithouse they lived in to excrete. With his powers he turned the excrement into a small tree. A beautiful bird sat on one of the branches. Coyote went back inside and said to his son, 'Come son, come see this beautiful bird sitting on top of that tree. It will be very nice to take to your son – it'll be a nice toy for him.'

The young man came out and looked up at the bird in the tree. He thought, 'That is a nice bird!' and he decided to climb up the tree to fetch it. He had just about got hold of it when Coyote used his powers again to make the tree grow taller and taller, until it reached the heavens. All the while his son was climbing. Finally, he reached the bird. As he grabbed it, the bird turned back into excrement. As Coyote's son was now in another world, old Coyote pulled away the tree.

The people in the pithouse asked old Coyote, 'Where's your son?'

Coyote said, 'Oh, I don't know. He was climbing the tree to catch that bird.'

Coyote's son's wives waited and waited for him to return. Old Coyote wanted his son's wives. The wife with the boy would not have anything to do with old Coyote, but he took the other wife for himself, as he planned.

Coyote's son was now all alone in the upper world, wandering about, lonely, and not knowing what to do next. He came upon a pithouse. Smoke was rising from it. He thought, 'Oh! I've come to some people. Oh, good!' He looked down into the opening. He said into the hole, 'Are you down there, my friends?' He repeated his question over and over. No one said anything, so he climbed down the ladder. When he got down, there was a small fire burning.

In those times, old people use to make combs from wood. There were wooden combs piled up all around the room.

He thought to himself, 'I wonder where everyone is? Oh, I'll just take one of these combs for myself.' He took one, looked it over, and said, 'This is a good one. It's going to be my comb.' He was going to go. As he was leaving, all the other combs clung onto him. He said to them, 'Oh, my friends! You are people! I will return your friend!' So he put the comb back where he got it, and the other combs went back to their places. He said goodbye to them and left.

Once again he was on his way, not knowing where he was. He went on and on until he came to another pithouse. Smoke was rising from it. 'Oh! I've come to some people!' said the young man. He spoke down the opening of the house and said, 'Anyone down there, my friends? I was wandering around and found you.' No one answered him. He spoke again. Still no one answered him. He spoke again. Still no one said anything. So he climbed down the ladder. He came upon lots and lots of blankets woven from bulrushes. The blankets were lying all over and all around the room. The young man said, 'The people must have gone away somewhere. Oh! I'm going to help myself to one of these blankets!' He looked them over and picked a nice one. He rolled up the blanket and was going to leave. As he was just about to climb up the ladder, all the other blankets wrapped themselves around him. He said to the blankets, 'Oh, my friends! You are people! I am going to return your friend!' He spread the blanket down on the floor. As he did this all the other blankets spread out in their places. He climbed up the ladder and said, 'Good-bye, my friends. I will be on my way now. I am just wandering around, getting lost.'

He walked and walked for a long time. He came to a place where he heard a noise, 'Tukw – tukw – tukw – tukw – tukw – tukw – tukw.'

'I wonder what that noise is?' he said.

'Tukw – tukw – tukw – tukw,' the noise continued as he walked along.

The noise was getting closer and closer, until he came to an old couple sitting on the side of the road. This old couple were grouse. They were hammering and grinding food. The 'Tukw – tukw – tukw – tukw' came from them. They were both blind. The young man sat beside them – he sat and watched the old couple.

Blue Grouse would grind and hammer away and say, 'Put out your hand,' and would pour food into Fool Hen's palm.

Fool Hen would pour it into her mouth and say, 'M-m-m-m, that's good!' Then Fool Hen would grind away. She felt around and said, 'Where is your hand? Put out your hand,' and poured food into Blue Grouse's hand. Blue Grouse poured it into his mouth.

All the time the younger man was watching them. He realized the old people were both blind. He thought, 'Oh, I'm going to take that away from them!'

Blue Grouse felt around for his food, then Fool Hen felt around for her food and said, 'Well! Where is it?'

Blue Grouse said, 'You took it!'

'No!' said Fool Hen.

'But there was a hand there!' said Blue Grouse.

'No! I didn't take it!' said Fool Hen.

Blue Grouse said, 'Hm-m-m-m, I smell someone's odour.' Fool Hen got really angry and threw Blue Grouse down and said, 'May your grandchildren hunt you and eat you! You will also peck on trees and you won't smell anyone any more!' Today only Blue Grouse is hunted and eaten.

The young man went on his way. Another old couple had already sensed the young man coming and busied themselves spinning twine.

The young man went on for a long way. Finally, he saw smoke. 'Oh! I've come to some people!' the young man thought to himself. There was a pithouse with smoke rising from it. He lowered his head into the entrance and saw two old people sitting inside and spinning twine.

'Come here. Come here son, come here. Your grandpa and I

have been busy making twine,' said the grandmother.

Grandpa said, 'Make your grandson something to eat. He must be hungry, the poor child.' These old people already knew what his father, Coyote, had done to this young man. The grandmother made some food for him to eat.

'We are making lots of twine,' said the grandmother. 'We know your father has been very bad. That is the reason we are spinning! Tomorrow, you are to go and bathe. Every morning you are to go into the sweathouse to cleanse yourself,' said the grandmother. The young man did – every morning he took a sweatbath. He mourned for his family – he was sad and lonely.

His grandpa told him, 'I have a bow and arrow. I used it when I was a young person. It's all there. You can go hunting with it.'

The young man was still sad thinking about his family and what his father, Coyote, had done to him. Grandpa said to him, 'Alright son, come here. Here is a large container with a lid.' Grandpa opened it and told him, 'Come here and take a look at your people.' He looked and saw his wives and son. Grandpa said, 'See your wife and son there? But Coyote has taken your other wife. This is the reason we are spinning lots of twine. You are going home – we are sending you home.'

The young man became very happy. He bathed and hunted every day. He did this for a long time. One day, he plucked four hairs and threw them across the spring. They became twine plants – sp'áts'en [hemp]. They were tall, healthy plants. He plucked some sp'áts'en and brought it to his grandmother. He asked his grandparents, 'Is this the plant you are using to make twine?'

'Yes! It is wonderful! Where did you find the sp'áts'en?' asked the grandpa.

The young man said, 'Oh, I got it at the place where I've been bathing.'

He hunted while his grandmother dried the meat. They had plenty put away. The old people owned a very huge round basket with a secure lid. 'Okay, I think this is good enough to get you down to where you are going. We're going to try it out,' said the grandmother. Now she transformed the pounds and pounds of dried meat and lard into four small bags. 'Now when you need this food, all you do is shake it and it will come back to its original size. Alright now, let's get you into the basket, but don't you ever open your eyes! You will go along until you reach the sky. You will land there and stop, but do not open your eyes! You will roll around, then fall four times. You will stop four times. Don't open your eyes at any time! The fourth time you land, you will roll around and you will hear a crow – then you can open your eyes!' said the grandmother.

The young man agreed, 'Okay, okay!'

The grandmother gave him his four small bags of meat and lard. She told him, 'Alright, get into the basket.' The grandfather and the grandmother sat side by side and proceeded to lower the young man down in the huge basket, singing, 'zíxa, zíxa, zíxa, zíxa [down, down, down, down].'

He was going lower and lower until he landed. He rolled about, then he thought, 'I'm going to see what happens if I open my eyes.' He opened his eyes. Up he went – right back to where he came from.

The grandparents told him, 'Don't you do that! You will never get home – you will never see your son again!'

The young man said, 'Oh, I was just testing it out! Alright, I will be on my way.'

Again the grandparents put him in the huge basket. They secured the lid and sang, 'zíxa, zíxa, zíxa, zíxa,' until he landed on the sky. The young man rolled around until he fell. He landed on the clouds. Not opening his eyes, he fell a second time. In the meantime, his grandparents were singing, 'zíxa, zíxa, zíxa, zíxa.' Finally, he landed on the top of a tree. He rolled around until he fell a third time. This time he landed on the tips of the grass. He rolled about until he fell again. This being the fourth time, he heard a crow cawing. 'Oh! I'm at the bottom!' he said. He lifted off the lid of the basket and looked around. He said, 'This is my country!' He was very happy. He put the lid back on the basket and took off.

This place where the young man landed is in Lytton. That is why a lot of people say Lytton must be the centre of the world – because all legends seem to meet there. Today, somewhere in Lytton is the flat rock where Ntl'ík'semtm landed.

The grandparents said, 'Oh, our grandson has landed!' These old people are the spiders with their web.

When the young man landed on earth, there was no one around. He went towards the Thompson River. He said to himself, 'How will I be able to cross over the river?' He saw some tl'úxwen̓ [horsetail plants] that could be pulled apart. He took one and split it apart. Then he broke a small stick and wedged it into the centre of the weed. He threw it into the water and it became a canoe. He took another piece and made an oar. He sat in the canoe and paddled across the Thompson River. When he landed, he packed his canoe to the shore and turned it over. This place is now called Ts'ek̲7awlhák̲s and is shaped like a canoe. It is located across the Thompson River from Lytton, beside the CNR tracks and the powerhouse. Before the CNR went through and partially destroyed it, this piece of land looked exactly like a ts'ek̲7áwlh [canoe].

From there he went to Petáni [Botanie] Valley. Following his family, he ran and laughed. He was very happy knowing he was going to find them soon.

The young man's wife came from a very poor family – maggots, beetles, and the like. She stayed with the old people, far from everyone. She was always sad and cried a lot – she never mingled with anyone.

On her way to Petáni with her son strapped on her back, she was sad, lonely, and crying. The boy turned back and started saying, 'Papa! Papa!'

'Oh, hush! Your father is long gone! We don't know where he is or what has happened to him!' said the mother.

But the boy continued to call out, 'Papa! Papa!'

The boy's mother stopped and looked back – she didn't see anyone. She kept going, then stopped and looked back again. The place where she did this is called Nek̲'na7k̲'í7x. At this place, a few of the trees are twisted back. The boy's mother looked back again, but still she didn't see anyone. Her husband waved at her over and over. Then she saw him. She exclaimed, 'Oh, you're back! I'm so happy you're back!'

Her husband said, 'Sit down on this rock.' Today this rock is still there, on the way to Petáni. The young man told his wife, 'This is what I brought.' He took a small bag of meat and shook it. The meat multiplied enough to go around and there was enough for his wife's family and all the old people. Everyone feasted. The young man told his wife, 'Do as you've always done. Always stay away from everyone. Live far from the people – you and your friends stay away from everyone.' Remember, his wife and her people were insects.

The woman and her friends agreed, 'Alright, we'll do that.' After the feast the people took off. The woman, her friends, and the old people made camp far from everyone else.

One evening, Crow came by. He thought, 'My in-laws seem very different. I'm going to see them. Maybe the wife has a man around.' He went in looking around. 'I'm looking around just to see how you're doing,' Crow told the wife. He hadn't seen the young man yet. The young man waved his hands at Crow's eyes, then Crow began to see him. Crow exclaimed, 'Oh, you've come home, my dear! You've come home!'

'Yes, I've come home,' the young man answered.

'We are so pitifully poor!' said Crow. 'We have hunted and hunted, but no luck! We are starving – your people are starving! We don't have anything to eat!'

The young man brought out one of his small bags of food. He shook it and it multiplied. The young man gave Crow some meat and some fat. He told him, 'Wait until everyone is quiet and asleep before you feed your children. Do not let anyone know about this.'

Crow went home. He waited until everyone was asleep, then he cut up the food and gave some to his four children. The people lived in a summer dwelling, which they shared – a few people stayed in one place.

The youngest of the children was so hungry, he gobbled down his food and started to choke. Old Coyote heard the noise. He got up and said, 'What is going on here?' He saw the younger child choking and nearly dying. Coyote stepped on the child's throat and out came his food. Coyote grabbed it and ate it. Remember, old Coyote is the young man's father. Coyote yelled, 'Where did you get this food?'

'Oh, I found it!' said Crow.

'No, you didn't just find this somewhere! This is good food! Where did you get it?' Coyote was just about to beat Crow.

'Ah, alright! The young man is back! Ntl'ík'semtm is back! I was over at their house and he gave me some meat and fat!' said Crow. He just about got a beating from Coyote.

In the meantime, Ntl'ík'semtm had herded all the deer to another country. No one was able to shoot any and the people were starving.

Old Coyote pretended that he was happy to see his son. He said, 'Oh, I'm so happy you've come!'

Coyote had one of his son's wives. Old Coyote told her, 'You had better go back to your husband.'

The young man, Coyote's son, said, 'No, you stay away from me! Stay with Coyote! I do not want you any more!'

The young man went hunting and shot lots and lots of deer. He told everyone, 'Go help yourselves. There is lots of meat out there.'

The young man decided to get even with his father, old Coyote. He gutted a deer and strung out the guts and jumped over it. The deer guts turned into a beautiful pack-strap. He picked it up and brought it to Coyote. He handed it to Coyote and told him, 'Why don't you go and pack some venison? I'm going to lend you my pack-strap.' It was a beautiful pack-strap.

'Oh, alright,' said Coyote, and he took off to where the deer were in piles and everyone was skinning them. Coyote, feeling very proud, took some long ribs. Coyote piled the ribs neatly and bundled them up with his son's pack-strap. He put the bundle on his back. He walked on a log that crossed a creek at Wísiyem̓xw [High Mountain]. Halfway across his pack-strap snapped in half. He grabbed his deer ribs, tied them together, and continued to cross the creek. The strap broke again and again. Finally, he fell off the log and into the creek, and he drifted away until he reached the Thompson River. Coyote turned himself into a board and floated and floated until he reached the mouth of the Fraser River at the Pacific Ocean.

There he came upon four women. The women, with their fish weir, were there to get a supply of salmon. They baked salmon over an open fire. The youngest of the sisters saw a board floating along and said, 'Oh! That driftwood will make a nice dish for us!'

The older sister told her, 'Oh, don't touch that thing! It has to be something not nice!' She already had a feeling that this was a trick.

'But that is going to make a nice dish for our roast salmon,' said the youngest sister. She picked it up anyway.

When they were ready to eat, they filled their dish with salmon. With their eyes closed, they said prayers. They opened their eyes and the roast was all finished. The older sister said, 'See! I said there was something queer about that driftwood!' They filled the dish again, said a yámit [prayer], opened their eyes, and the same thing happened. The older sister got very angry, grabbed the wood, and threw it into the fire. From the flames came a baby's cry, 'Wa, wa, wa!' Coyote had changed into a baby.

'Quick,' said the women, 'Grab the baby away from the fire! Oh! It's a baby boy! Ooooo, we'll bring him up! We'll take good care of him! He's going to be a good helper when he gets older!' Remember, this baby is really Coyote. The women made a nice swing for the boy.

There were four great big round baskets that the women owned. All of them contained something. One contained bees, another contained flies, another contained the wind, and the fourth contained fog. These baskets had secure lids.

The women always went out to do something – most of the

time they prepared and preserved food. Every day one woman would stay at home to take care of the boy. He grew very fast, and was already running around. The youngest woman said, 'Why don't we bring the boy with us? This way one of us won't always have to stay home any more. He is strong enough to come with us.' The boy was frolicking around.

The following day they brought the boy with them. He started to fuss. The youngest woman picked him up and packed him on her back. They all took turns packing the boy. Finally they got tired of packing him all the time, so they decided to leave him home. They told the little boy, 'See these baskets? You are not to touch them; and don't go near the river, you might drown! Stay away from the fish weir!' The weir was between the river and the ocean.

The boy agreed, 'Alright, alright, I'll stay!'

The women would go out to work, and when they returned, everything would be fine. Now one time they were going somewhere for four days. They told the boy to never touch the four baskets and to keep away from the river.

The boy waited until the women were long gone, then he said, 'Oh, I am going to go home. I am leaving these women.' Then he decided, 'Oh, I'm going to see what is in these baskets.' First he opened the bees and the flies, then he opened the baskets with the wind and fog. The wind blew the flies and bees everywhere, then it fogged up. The four sisters realized what had happened when they saw the results of the opened baskets. They tried to gather the insects, but couldn't do much because of the fog and the wind.

Meanwhile, the boy pulled on the fish weir and went across and stood on the other side of the river. He enjoyed watching the four sisters trying to gather up the insects. He hollered over to the women, 'Good-bye! Good-bye!'

Now the salmon were freed from the ocean and went up the Fraser River by the hundreds. This is how salmon came to be in the Fraser River.

As Coyote was going home, he felt hungry. He took out a

salmon, and when he had finished eating it, he gave the salmon a name – also the fishing place. He did this all the way up the Fraser River. That is why all the fishing places have names and the salmon have different names. He did this all the way to the joining of the two rivers – the Thompson and the Fraser.

Coyote and His Son

Told by Walter Isaac
Translated by Mamie Henry

THIS STORY is about Coyote. Coyote told his daughters-in-law to take a bath, and he told his son to go and hunt. He told his daughters-in-law again, 'Take your bath.' Coyote had already taken a liking to his daughters-in-law, who were ducks. One was black and the other white. The white duck was the one Coyote admired; she was a slender, young white duck.

The daughters-in-law took their baths while Coyote kept the fire stoked. It got hot and sparks flew on the behinds of the ducks. Coyote looked on. The black one was all black and ugly while the white one was all nice and white. 'Oh, that's the one I'm going to take!' said Coyote, referring to the white duck.

'When my son returns he's going to climb up that tree. Up there is a robin. He is going to take it and use it,' Coyote thought to himself. When Coyote's son returned, Coyote told him, 'You are going to the top of that tree. There is a bird up there, and you are going to use its feathers.'

So Coyote's son climbed up to the top of the tree. In the meantime, his father encouraged the boy to keep going. He went up, up, up, and up until he reached the sky. He poked his head through the clouds and exclaimed, 'I'm in another world!'

He walked until he came to a house. This was the house of Grouse and his blind wife. From there, he kept on until he got to where Spider was busy making twine for a huge round net. Coyote's son said, 'That will take a very long time to fill.' He plucked out four of his hairs and flung them down. They turned into a length of twine – it was as long as twine can get. 'Now I can go home,' thought Coyote's son.

The next morning the net was full. Said the grandfather Spider, 'When the net is full again, we are going to dangle you down to the earth. We're going to dangle you far down.'

'This is how it is going to go,' the grandfather continued. 'When you get there, you are going to roll about on the treetops. From there you are going to fall down and reach the bushes and you are going to roll about. Then you will reach the tops of the grass and you will again roll about. Finally, you will fall onto the earth. Then you may open your eyes.'

The boy was lowered down, down, down, down until he reached the land of trees. He opened his eyes and he was right back up where he came from. 'What's wrong?' asked Spider, 'Why did you open your eyes so soon?'

'Oh, I'm just saying "so long" to you,' said the boy. 'I'm happy that you are sending me home!'

So they tried again. Down, down, down, down went the boy. When he reached the treetops he rolled about. He reached the bushes and he opened his eyes. Again he returned to his starting point. Grandfather Spider was angry with him. 'What's wrong?' he demanded.

'Oh, I'm just bidding you goodbye! I'm glad you're sending me home!' said the boy.

The boy was lowered for a third time. This time he reached the grasslands before he opened his eyes. Once more he found himself back with Spider.

'Its the fourth time!' said Spider. 'Now it's the earth! You are to stop four times before you open your eyes! Alright now, down.'

Down, down, down, down went the boy, until he reached the treetops. He rolled about. He fell again, this time to the bushes.

Again he rolled about. Then he fell to the grass and rolled about. Finally he fell to the bottom, the earth, and opened his eyes. He had reached his home, the Petáni Valley.

'Where are my wives?' Coyote's son wondered. They and everyone else had gone up the hills to dig roots. The boy was angry – he was very angry. He was treading on maggots, which were splashing on his feet. The maggots said to him, 'You are mistreating us! We are going up the hills too!'

'You are the boy that was sent up to the sky, aren't you?' asked the maggots. They had already heard about him.

The young man left his home in search of his wives and father, asking the people where they were. 'They went that way, or perhaps that way – up Wísiyem̓xw [High Mountain],' they told him.

Finally the young man found his wife – the black one. 'Where is my father?' he asked her.

'Oh, he's already taken your other wife,' she said.

'Well, where are they?' he demanded.

'Downstream a bit,' she answered.

The young man then went hunting. He shot a deer across the water, where he left it. He braided the intestines, which he took home with him. When he had finished the braid, he gave it to his father so he could pack the ribs. 'That's what I left for you,' he said, 'and this is a pack-strap for you.'

'This will serve you right,' the young man thought to himself. 'You are going to drown. You will be just halfway across; your strap will break and you will drown.' And that is what happened. As Coyote was packing the deer ribs, the strap broke while he was in the middle of the water.

As he was drowning, Coyote turned into a small board and floated to the edge of the water. There were some women there who said, 'Oh, here's a board! It will be our dish. We're going to take it.' And they took the little board home.

While the women were busy, the board turned into a young man. 'Oh!' the women exclaimed, 'he's going to be our husband!'

But Coyote only stayed for a short time and then left.

Coyote was now on his way to change the world. He made his way to Falls Creek, where he made a blockage. He made other blockages here and there all the way to Lytton. There he spied on a group of women bathing across the river. 'Oh!' he said, 'A lovely bunch of women!'

He hollered at them, 'How would you like to play ball with me? Send your youngest sister across!' When the young woman was halfway across, he threw the ball at her. She could not let go of it. She punched it and hammered it; but no, she could not get rid of it.

So Coyote went on his way until he reached Lillooet. There again he saw a bunch of women bathing across the river. 'Are you hungry for beaver?' he called.

'No, we're not hungry for beaver,' they replied. 'We're hungry for mountain goat.'

So again he made a ridge that no one could get over. From there he went downstream to where he had left his things with the young women. On his way he made himself a vest, hat, shoes, and coat. He made them out of the moss on the trees, which made very nice clothes.

Coyote went along until he reached the place where his wife was – Nx̱wu7mín [near Earlscourt, across from Lytton]. He began to make strange noises and signs with his hands. 'Tu!' he said, 'Tu! I know how to blow.'

'Oh!' the people said, 'he must be an Indian doctor!'

'There's a young girl sick here,' they told him. 'You doctor her.'

'Yeah' said Coyote.

'Blow, blow, blow,' said Blue Jay, the interpreter. 'He's an Indian doctor, alright!'

Once again Coyote made strange noises, and he made signs with his hands. 'Make it small; cover it up with things.'

The people got together and made a small sweathouse inside the pithouse. There Coyote began to perform his act, blowing and singing, becoming stranger and stranger. The sweathouse was bobbing up and down – Coyote was singing to his heart's content.

'What's going on here?' the people wondered. They opened the flap and there was Coyote – on top of the young girl.

The people attacked Coyote with shotguns and other weapons. Coyote leapt away from them, leaving his belongings still hanging there. His coat, his hat, and his shoes all turned into ashes, moss, and fir branches.

'Oh, those Coyotes! You people ought to kill them off – get rid of all of them!' said the old folks. 'They never have pity on us! But anyway, the sick girl is better. She is well again.'

The Trip to the Moon

Told by Annie York
Translated by Mamie Henry

AT ONE TIME, many people lived at Nweyts [Nooaitch/ Canford], where they would hunt mountain sheep. One day a man shot a mountain sheep, skinned it, and spread it out on wood to dry. He then built a fire, tied the skin together, and began to blow it up. He blew and blew. Suddenly, the skin exploded! It made such an explosion that the rocks were blown to pieces. That is why Nweyts is covered with shale today.

In the spring, the man decided to move to Nk̲'awmn [Nicomen]. He packed all his belongings and took his family to Nk̲'awmn, as there were lots of salmon at that place. The man had not forgotten what he had intended to do. So he tried to blow up another sheepskin. As he blew, he looked up at the sky and thought about the moon. 'Oh, there must be good land up there,' he thought to himself. The place where he was blowing up the sheepskin had a large, flat rock.

Finally, he was able to blow up a sheepskin into a large basket. He made a lid for it. He wanted very much to be able to go to the moon to see what type of people were living there, so he packed some food, a pair of moccasins, and his rifle. 'I'm going out for a walk,' he told his wife. He then put his belongings into the air basket.

To get the air basket moving, he had to run alongside it and then jump into it once it was airborne. Through the air he flew. Eventually, the air basket landed and the man lifted the lid and peeked out. There were pithouses all around him and smoke was coming out of the top of each. He entered one, but he couldn't see anyone; all he could see were basket reeds moving, and he could hear women talking. Baskets lined the walls of the house. As he reached over to pick one up, he was unable to stand up, and an old woman's voice said, 'Do not try to take one of those baskets or you will never be able to leave this place.' Quickly, the man left that pithouse and entered another.

He couldn't see anyone in this pithouse either, although he could hear voices. Beautiful mats and blankets were around the walls of the pithouse. He saw one mat that he was very fond of, so he began to take it down from the wall. Instantly, he was covered with mats, and again the voice said to him, 'Do not steal from us, as stealing is a bad thing to do. If you take that mat, you will never see your home again.' He hung the mats back on the wall.

The man entered another pithouse, where he saw lots of arrows, knives, stone hammers, and ammunition. There was also a packsack in this house, so he began to fill it with the various implements. All at once, everything fell on top of him and he received a black eye. 'Oh, these people are so mean to me!' he thought to himself as he lay on the floor.

'Never, never steal!' said the voice once again.

'Okay, I won't steal from you!' he replied.

Another person said to him, 'Now, you must do only what is right.'

He began to pick up the arrows and put them back in their place – but instantly, everything was back in its place.

The man left and travelled to where there was a little pithouse with a small pile of wood outside. He looked down the smoke-hole and saw a small fire and an old couple huddled around it trying to keep warm. 'Come in,' they called to him. 'I suppose you are just travelling around?'

'Yes,' answered the man, 'I have always wondered about this place. Where I live, it shines down on us.'

The old woman then told the young man a story. 'This is a very large land,' she explained, 'In the centre of the land there is a large mountain. A ship-shaped object stands on top of that peak. One day, a man just like you came to this land, and the people put a spell on him and changed him into a rock.' The old woman told the man to bring his belongings into the house and stay with them. 'There is nothing else for you to do, as you can no longer go home.'

The days went by and the young man provided for the old couple. He hunted and chopped wood for them. The old woman warned him never to visit the other people and, most important, never to steal from them. She explained that the people were invisible. The young man did exactly as he was told. For two years, he hunted and cared for the old people while they busied themselves making twine. They made balls and balls of twine – he wondered what they needed it for.

One night, the old woman said to the young man, 'You are very lonesome for your family. Every night I hear you weeping.'

'Yes,' replied the man, 'I miss my children.'

'We are almost finished our task and then you can go home,' the old woman told him. After she said this, the man felt better and went about his chores.

'Early in the morning, you will have to leave us!' sobbed the old woman. 'When you are gone we will be facing hard times again!' The old woman prepared a large meal and gave the man a sack of roots, berries, and meat to take back to his home. She also gave him a large pile of skins. In a sack, she gave him instructions for making baskets, tanning hides, and steaming roots. 'Give those to the women,' she told him. Then she gave him some instructions for teaching the men how to make arrowheads, how to dry salmon, and how to make snowshoes. 'We want you to teach the people everything that we have taught you.'

Suddenly the man felt sad about leaving the old people behind. They gave him a new, fancy air basket and packed up all his gifts. Once he climbed inside, the old woman gave the young man a stone hammer and told him to keep tapping the bottom of the basket. 'When you hear a solid noise, you will know that you have reached your world. First, you will hit the sky and then some other things, but, eventually, you will reach the ground.' Just as she closed its lid, one of the old woman's tears rolled from her cheek and dropped into the basket.

The old people ran with the basket until it started to go. One end of the rope was tied to the man's waist and the other end was tied to the basket. 'Lower, lower, lower, lower,' he sang. The basket glided through the air.

The young man tapped the bottom of the basket when he reached the sky, but because it wasn't solid, he realized that he was not home on earth yet. He threw off the lid of the basket and looked around to discover that he was in Nk̲'awmn.

He unloaded all the gifts that the old woman had given him. As he had to return the basket to the moon, he followed the instructions that the old people had given him. He closed the lid and, as he did so, a tear dropped from his cheek into the basket. Then he ran with it and let it fly into the air. A voice spoke to him and said, 'You are crying too, just as we did when you left our land. From this day on, people will cry. And the world will cry, and the people will call it "rain."'

It was springtime on earth. As he climbed up the path towards the houses, the people called to each other and asked who the stranger was. At first they thought that it was an enemy, but his face wasn't painted. Then they recognized who it was, and the woman told her children to greet their father. It had been a long time since they had seen him, and the children didn't know the man until their mother told them who he was.

The woman prepared a large meal and everyone ate. Then the man took out his gifts and showed them to his wife. 'We eat our food raw, but in the land where I was visiting, they cook their food. Here is some dried meat, and these roots are steamed.' Because the people had never used a fire, he had to gather some jack-pine wood and some cottonwood and show them how to make a fire by rubbing two sticks together. A spark fell on some dry grass and he made a fire. When the fire was hot, he took out the birch-bark basket that he had been given, filled it with water, and dropped a hot rock into it. Suddenly the water began to boil and the man cooked some meat. His wife stood over him and watched in amazement. He then rolled out a mat and put the cooked meat on top of it. After he had spread out the rest of the food, he told his wife to call together all of the people. They were surprised with the gifts that the old people had given the man and listened eagerly as he explained to them how they were to be used. All the people learned what the man had been taught while he was on the moon.

One day, the young man gazed up at the moon and someone spoke to him. 'There is no one up there now,' said the voice, 'but some day, people will again go up there. They won't find it the same, for everything is gone.'

Coyote and the Three Sisters

Told by Louie Phillips

THREE SISTERS were walking across the Fraser River – one young, one middle-aged, and one old. Coyote was caught up on the east side with a green pack. He saw these girls over there and he asked them, 'Are you hungry?' But he had nothing to eat. What he was packing was his privates. He had to roll it up, put green boughs on it, and pack it. When he was down there he said he would untie it.

These little girls didn't know what it was. They ask their older sister, 'What did he say? What did he say?'

The old one said, 'I'm going to keep quiet.' She really wanted to know what Coyote was offering.

He threw it across the river and he nailed the little girl. The little girl was going to be dragged right into the river, but the other two were pulling and pulling – they were sliding in.

Then Coyote tells them, 'There's only one type of grass that cuts that.' There is a little swamp up there, above the apple-packing house. One of the girls ran up to the swamp, cut a piece of blade grass, and came back. They just touched it and it cut off. He coil it up and left. And this girl is nailed – a piece of Coyote's privates is in there. The next day, the girl was sick – dying. I didn't hear where Coyote crossed the river to come down to get that piece out of the girl.

That girl was dying – her parents were afraid that she was going to die. They hired all the Indian doctors. They find it was Coyote that did it. That piece is in her, and that's what's going to kill the girl.

But he went across the river up there some place. He came back. He didn't go to the girl's parents – he went in with another Indian family. The kids were playing around there. He seen this old man in there and he pretend to be different. He talked.

There's an old man there, and he says, 'Maybe you're a doctor?'

And these people here are afraid they're going to lose their daughter. So they run over there and talk to Coyote, 'You come and talk – our daughter's dying!' But that's what he was coming for – he went over there. They said, 'The young girl there is sick. We don't know what to do with her.' And he made it so the doctors could not find it. He got in there and they said to him, 'Girl's sick, very sick.'

But he's going to use the girl to get that thing reconnected and get it out of there. He told the people, 'I will put a little cover over so people don't watch when I doctor.' And he made a shade out of bulrushes – you know, that grow in swamps. They put that over so they can't see. Coyote went in and started singing.

And one old man says, 'His wife, I'm going to get her. She will tell us what he's singing.' Little Mole was Coyote's wife. So they ran and they got Little Mole, and the old man said, 'Listen, we can't make out what he's saying.' He stopped talking. Coyote made it impossible for anyone to understand. They asked his wife, 'What is he saying? What does he mean to say?'

'Oh,' she says, 'that's Senk'iy̓áp [Coyote]. He's just funny, acting funny. He's the one that got the girl sick, so sick that she's going to die.'

Of course Coyote's tool is in her and it's getting spoiled, getting rotten. His wife told on him and he put a cover over the girl. He got in there and started singing, and he was using the girl. When he got it reconnected, he said, 'Alright, all over. Take the covers off.' They take the covers off. He's part connected – he's got the piece back that was killing the girl.

The parents ask, 'How long before the girl will be better?'

'Oh,' he says, 'tomorrow, sun-up, she'll be running around, jumping around, like there was nothing wrong with her.' So the people kind of wait for her. Sun-up, the girl got up, started playing, running around. Couple of days later, there was nothing wrong with her.

I guess they were going to kill Coyote, but he made it so nobody knew where he went. Ah, he's a dirty bugger!

Coyote and Wolf

Told by Herb Manuel

THIS STORY IS ABOUT Coyote and his brother, Wolf. There is a special ball that the Lytton people used to play with. Coyote and Wolf planned to get it.

I want to tell you about Coyote's character first. When the big flood was on, Coyote had a boat. When he landed, he was the only person around. I guess somebody with a stronger power than he has gave him the job of going about and straightening this world, because what was going to happen was all going to be bad. There was going to be a lot of bad things – a lot of bad going on in the world that he had to go and straighten out. His character was so weird. He had the power to do all things, and yet he was mischievous. He would do things wrong – just knowingly he would get killed. He was daring – he dared the powers of other things. But the person who gave him that job gave him a brother, which was Fox, and told him, 'Whenever you are old and the power in you dies, if one hair is found by Fox, he'll step over it four times and you'll come alive again.' In a lot of cases, Coyote would challenge something and he would be overpowered and killed, but he would return to life and transform whatever had killed him into what it is now, more or less. In his travels he was always somewhere near Fox. Fox would rescue him.

This one mission Coyote had, he had four sons and he lived in Merritt and he had a brother, Wolf. The people from the south say it was Antelope, but the people here say it was Wolf. Wolf would more likely be his brother.

The Lytton people had a ball, which they played with. There was kind of a weekend festival they would have every so often. They would have a great time playing with this ball. People came from miles around; all the Nlha7kápmx would go there and enjoy themselves. Coyote went down there.

Coyote was a show-off. He was kind of always undernourished. He was, in human flesh, a skinny, tall man with drawn-in cheeks, and when he spoke, he spoke with a drawn-in voice. He spoke funny. You knew it was him when you heard his voice. He spoke this way. There was no way he could get away from his speech.

Anyway, he came back and told his brother, Wolf, 'I'm going to train my sons. I'm going to go down and get the ball and bring it up here to the Nicola Valley.'

Wolf told his brother, 'No, those people are quite strong. You can't just go down there with those four skinny little guys.'

All his kids were very undernourished. Each one had a crazy name. All their names were all around their back end like Kelhtatálheṅk̲wa7, Yi7ánek̓nlháwstn, Nk'iyápaplhxw. Síswa7 was the younger one. They had those names because they used to have the runs – it was always on their behind. And one, Yi7ánek̓nlháwstn, his hind legs were so weak that when he walked he would wobble.

So together they practised. Wolf agreed that his brother would go with him, and daily the sons practised. Coyote's family practised up the Nicola and up towards Coyote Valley. They practised all over in there for days on end, and towards the very end they would sweat – and they had a special diet they were going on. Just like they were going for an Olympic event.

The Wolves, in the meantime, practised through the rough terrain above Nicola Lake, through this way [Douglas Lake], back towards the Coquihalla. They practised in rough terrain where it was rocky because they knew that the Lytton Valley was rocky country.

Coyote had his kids out there on the flat country – where it was easy going. Where they were supposed to be training, those kids would run over the hill. And they were not supposed to eat, but they'd run across some berries and they'd cheat and eat away and get fat and lay around. They'd be lazy or cheating all the time – they were like their dad. Anyway, they practised for one full year, through the summer months and through the winter. They made out that they were in top-notch shape. Now they were ready to go for the ball.

Their house was right at the King Garden Manor [Merritt]. Right at the King Garden Manor there was a low-lying mountain – a little hill. I've seen it. It's called Senk'iy̓apáplhxw – Coyote's House. That house was pure gravel, and they used it to pave the road from Merritt, up the Nicola, to Sulús [Shulus], and up towards Princeton Road – as far as they could while the gravel lasted. It was pea gravel. The hill was beautiful and it was shaped just like a loaf of bread. And it was about two hundred yards to three hundred yards in length. That was his house. The town of Merritt, or the government, or the highways, or whatever levelled it. That was where he lived. Coyote had a sweathouse and it is still visible. It is across the river. It is about twelve feet on the outside, and the rock formation would be about two feet thick – perfectly round as a sweathouse. That was Coyote's sweathouse – it is still there.

Anyway, on that day they were going down, and they had a meeting. Coyote insisted his boys were better than the Wolf boys, and he said, 'Okay I will take my boys way down and we will get the ball. I will send my best boy – the youngest – to pick up the ball, and he will run up the river and he will throw it across; and the other guy will pick it up and he will run up the river and, if he never gets caught, he will throw it across to his brother, and his brother will relay it.' So they had three relays to go.

So they were down there and they were playing with this ball. There would be a line of players in the middle, and another line away from the middle. There were many teams, and they would throw this ball back and forth, and the guys in the middle would throw the ball. If you caught the ball, your team would then go back in the middle. The team in the middle would be disqualified and another team would take its place trying to catch the ball.

Anyways, they went down there. The youngest Coyote, Síswa7, got in the ball game because they had the power to change themselves into whatever they wanted to. The relayers changed themselves into rocks so they weren't seen. Presently, the Wolf wanted to take that area, but the Coyote argued continuously, argued for that position, and the Wolf boys took the other positions. These boys started from Spences Bridge up the Nicola River. Coyote sat on a hill up above Spences Bridge and watched his boys. He cheered for them from up the hill.

The boy who caught the ball just threw it, and he was caught there and slain. Some Nlha7kápmx on that side pursued him, and just as he threw the ball he was caught and slain. Same with this guy. Every time they just threw the ball, they would be caught and slain. So all the Coyote kids were slain, and the last one passed the ball over to one of the Wolf kids, and he out-ran the Lytton people.

He threw the ball back and forth, like that, then he disappeared into the wilderness and he came home. So he got home – and Coyote, well, he went back and looked – his kids were sure enough dead. He knew they were dead. He was broken-hearted, and yet, being who he is, he still had some cocky feelings in his mind. He was going to avenge the deaths of his boys, so he came up and he pouted around in the lodge there.

The boys were quite proud of the ball. They rolled it around, kicked it about, and played with it. It was a huge ball – it was bright. Well, by the description it might have been three feet in diameter, and it was a bright shiny object and light enough to be thrown or kicked. It floated. Anyway, they had the toy that belonged to the Nlha7kápmx. So they kicked it about there for three days, and on the fourth night Coyote went and he pleaded with his brother. He said, 'I am in deep sorrow. My children were slain on the journey we took to get that ball. They lost their lives for that ball and I made a mistake – your children may have been a little wiser, but I put my children in front. That's how much love I have for your boys. Your boys are now alive. I weakened their main line before they reached you. I would like to take the ball and put it under my head for the night and just weep on it in the memory of my boys.'

So Wolf gladly told him, 'Okay.'

Coyote took the ball, and he done this for four nights. On the fourth night he blew something over his brother and his sons. Blew over them and they fell asleep – slept longer than they regularly do. He took the ball down to about Spences Bridge. He broke the ball up – he busted it up and it turned into a shell – a shell which was unpierceable. By the description, maybe it was one and a half to two inches in thickness. And Coyote changed himself into an elk. Then he put armour all around him, everywhere. He patched himself all around so no arrows or anything could pierce him, and he sharpened his horns and hooves to be knife sharp. (If you see a coyote and an elk now, there's a little white spot right under their throat; and just down at their rectum is another little white spot.)

He was going down to clean up on the Nlha7kápmx of Lytton.

Anyways, he went down there at night. In the morning the people got up and they saw the big elk on the hillside there, and everybody said, 'Hey, there's an elk up there! Let's go up and shoot him!' Everybody got out their arrows and headed up there, and they shot at him, and the arrows just bounced off him, and he came down into the village. He just killed a whole bunch of them, and he was killing the people as he went along. He was taking revenge on the people. They were trying to jump on him, club him, spear him, and everything. He was killing as he was going along, with his horns and hooves.

The Meadowlark is always the tattle-tale bird. Events like this, he always told on somebody. He landed on a pole, outside of the village and he spoke in Nlha7kapmxtsín, 'Tsukw tl'u7 a sk'emálhxwi7ts, Tsukw tl'u7 a sk'emálhxwi7ts [Only his Adam's apple. Only his Adam's apple] Tsukw tl'u7 a np'u7tns [Only his behind].'

The old people listened – they said, 'Hey, he's telling us something!'

He said it again, 'Tsukw tl'u7 a sk'emálhxwi7ts. Tsukw tl'u7 a np'u7tns.'

Then one old man said, 'I got it! Just here – just at his Adam's apple, there's an opening; and down at his rear-end, there's an opening. He must get an arrow in there or a spear.' He told some of the young people, 'Try for that spot right there.' So they got him, and they finally killed old Coyote. The ball disappeared there, and of course Coyote died with the ball – but he nearly wiped out the Nlha7kápmx because of that ball. Later on, his brother, the Fox, jumped over him and a new story begins.

Coyote and Buffalo

Told by Herb Manuel

COYOTE WAS TRAVELLING BY one day, just bored. There was nobody around – absolutely nothing around there, and he was hungry. He's always hungry. Seen these pile of bones – buffalo bones – one pile, just the way he died. No scavenger took anything – it was all there, just the way he died. He died fighting for his wives years ago.

So Coyote, he went by there and he sucked on all the bones. He sat down. He got the two ribs and he started beating on them. He started singing, just making no sense. They say that's why you still hear Coyote, still singing around now and then. He does that all the time. He finds a pile of bones or something, or a smell of something dead, and he'll start singing like that again. And he rattled those bones.

And Buffalo told him, 'Oh, leave me alone! I've been dead here since a long time ago. Why don't you just go on your way? Can't you see I'm poor, all faded? Leave me alone.'

Coyote got singing louder. He got through singing and he looked at Buffalo – he laughed at old Buffalo laying there. So Coyote rested his foot on the pile of bones.

And that was all Buffalo needed. He put himself back together – he was just bones. He told Coyote, 'I'm going to kill you, Coyote.'

'What are you talking about, you're going to kill me? You're just a rack of bones there.' So Coyote jogs on quite fast. He hears old Buffalo coming, 'Just, just, just, just, just, just!' Coyote was having a nap, and he looked there. Buffalo's right around over the next hill. He got away from the wind. This went on day and night – Buffalo chased Coyote. He had no peace. He went on and on and on. Pretty soon he was run out of strength. He had no water. He had nothing to eat for days on end because Buffalo bones was chasing him. And he was running with all his might. And he had to climb, and he got towards the top, and he couldn't go no further. He stopped and Buffalo was about to gore him, but he had no horns – he was just bony. He was going to bump him. Coyote said, 'Peace! Peace!' He said, 'Let's talk! I'll make you a deal. I'll fix you up, if you quit chasing me. I'll put you back together and you can go after your enemy. I'll fix you up the way you were – you'll be a young man again.'

Buffalo said, 'But if you lie, Coyote, I'm still going to kill you.'

So Coyote went to work and put him back together – built him stronger than ever. Coyote put thick fur, thick hair, thick skin all over Buffalo – built him just the way he is. But boy, he was just a little leaner!

And he said to him, 'Well, you have to have horns.' So they looked about at all the sticks. 'These pine branches here look about as strong as can be.' He gathered these pine branches, stuck them on Buffalo's head, and told him, 'We'll use that big pine tree there to practise on. You take a run at it. See if it sticks, so it won't break.'

He ran, he hit that thing, and Whamo! – the branches were broken.

'No, we have to find a stick here. Something has got to work.' And he tried the fir tree. That didn't work. Then he thought for a while. He said, 'Well, maybe something a little harder.'

He tried a birch. Birch is hard wood, but it didn't work. He tried that. No. They were trying out horns, the Buffalo and Coyote, and they tried out all the sticks they could find. They were getting disgusted, and Coyote's life was at stake.

So they tried ts'itl' [pitch] from a dead fir tree – an old dead fir tree, pretty well petrified. The pitch would be just black – really solid and hard; but it burns easy. You could make a spear out of it, it's so hard. It's really good wood, and it won't break so easy. So they tried this ts'itl' – pitch for his horns. Took a run at that pine tree and it stuck. He backed up and hit it again – it stuck. And Coyote said, 'That's the one we're looking for! Yes!'

They were quite happy and Coyote told Kwesp – that's Buffalo in the Okanagan language, 'Let's go down to the lake. Have a look at yourself. See your image in the water – it's a looking-glass.' So he walked down and looked at himself. Ah, he was happy at how he looked! He was satisfied!

'Okay Coyote,' he said, 'now that you fixed me up, I'm going to fix you up.'

They say Coyote at that time had big ugly feet – very big feet, ugly and clumsy – and he had a smashed-in face from fighting so much. He had a little short nose, like a bulldog, and floppy ears and a little short stubbed tail – he had a long back and he had short legs, like a baloney dog.

Buffalo told him, 'I'll pretty you up too, partner.' Grabbed him by the ears – like that. Got his nose and stretched it a couple of times. Held it for a while – let him go. He had a nice, long nose. Stretched his eyes back a little, pulled his tail out and fluffed it up a little bit. Pulled his legs out – made nice, cute, small feet on him so he could run faster. Shortened his body up, give him better fur. 'Okay Coyote, go and have a look.' He had a look and he couldn't quit looking at himself. He would run back down there and turn around and pose for himself.

Anyways, 'I'm not quite through with you, Buffalo. I want to see you use them horns. I know where your enemy is. You still got your wives just over the mountain there,' he said. 'We'll go over there and you'll fight and get your wives back. You got all the equipment you need now,' he said. 'I sit up the hill and cheer for you. I ain't going to be part of the fight,' he said. 'Ah,' he said, 'if you get killed, I'll jump over you and bring you back to life – that way I'll owe you nothing.'

'Okay,' said Buffalo.

So they travelled over the hills and through the mountains and out to the Prairies. They came over this big hill, and there was a big herd of buffalo down there. There was a great big bull down there.

Coyote said, 'There's your enemy – kill him.'

Buffalo said to Coyote, 'Yes, I'll go fight now – kill him. But I'm going to wait until sunrise – make an event of it.'

So they sat on the hill and waited. Slept over night and waited for the sun to rise. When the sun rose they walked down, Buffalo let out a bellow of challenge, and the big bull, his enemy, came trolling out of the herd.

Buffalo hit him and they had a fight. They fought and fought. They went down – Coyote's friend went down a few times. Buffalo, when he would be right down, Coyote would give him a bracer with his power again and again, and he'd get back up – he'd get at it again. He finally got the best of that big bull, and he killed him and he took over the herd.

So Coyote travelled with his partner. They went around – they were friends for a few years.

And Buffalo told him, 'It's not right that you live with me and my kind. It's unfair for you to live with me.' He said, 'We will part. You go this way, I go that way; but before we part I'll give you one of my wives – not to be your wife, but to be your food.' He said, 'You can cut a chunk. You push her over anytime. Touch her – push her over like that. She'll fall over and she'll fall asleep.' He said, 'Take three or four slices out of the upper rear. When you have enough, slowly rub it over and it will heal and she'll get up and you guys can travel again. Every time you're hungry, you do it.' He said, 'Do it no more than two times a day, sunrise and sunset.'

Coyote was just over the hill, 'Gee, I got to try this out!' Gives her a push – down she went. Hacked a chunk out of her – three or four steaks out of the hind leg there. He cooked it up and ate. Then away he went. He was just barely over the hill there – and he pushed her down again. 'I'm hungry – I'm packing my lunch along. I'm far enough away from my partner – he don't know what date it is.' Down she went again.

It was getting shorter between times – it was getting tiresome.

So the next time he dropped a chunk, he had his friends around. The type of friends that he carried were low-grade. Always Raven and Crow and Magpie and those type of scavengers – those were his people. He invited them over, 'Come on down here,' he said, 'I got the real McCoy! Feast here! Get over here!' So they ate and got past the upper rear and, of course, old Raven, he wouldn't quit eating, and Magpie – they were fighting for it.

Crow said, 'I'm going to eat!'

Magpie would say, 'No, I'm going to eat!'

And they were fighting. Finally, they finished – ate the whole thing up. Coyote was trying to pull them off, and they were biting at him. They ate his wife all to nothing, so he couldn't put the skin back on and it was all dragged away – it was eaten. Just the bones were laying there. He was given trust that he broke. So that was the end of his glory.

Coyote and Wood Tick

Told by Herb Manuel

COYOTE WAS ALWAYS a poor hunter – he was absolutely no good at anything. He was hungry, walking along, and he seen smoke coming up. He edged his way along the rocks – got closer to the rocks. He could smell something – 'Fresh meat!' He changed himself from his ugly, usual self – he made himself presentable. He put on some clean clothes, walked over there, and asked, 'What are you doing?'

'Oh, I live here by myself – I eat a lot.' That was Wood Tick.

'Oh,' he said, 'let me help you with that meat you're skinning there. If I help you, will you let me eat with you?'

So he told him, 'Okay.'

So they started a fire, and Coyote went down to skin. Got the skin off, and they cooked the whole deer up and they ate it through the night. In the morning, Wood Tick went out to get another deer. Coyote told him, 'I'll tan these hides for you. All of these hides I'll tan for you, if you let me stay with you – just eat with you.'

'Okay, you can tan hides all you want, eat, go up the hill.' All Wood Tick had was his staff, and he went to this big bluff. At the bottom of this big bluff he would hit his staff on the ground. Down came a deer. It was dead. He took it home. Not long he was home, and Coyote was starting to get a little fatter.

Coyote, a little bit lively, 'Gee whiz, you know, big chief like you shouldn't drag that máwits [Chinook for deer] home like that! Let me go with you, see how you do it, and I'll drag the máwits! You're a big chief – you don't have to do anything!' So Coyote convinced him of that.

They went up there. Wood Tick struck the staff on the ground again. Down came a deer. Hauled it home – skinned it out. Coyote said, 'Lay down over there. I'll do the cooking, you're a big chief now – I know how to do all this now.' He did the cooking.

This went on pretty good for a while. Wood Tick was getting a little lazy, and Coyote was doing a pretty good job. He seemed to be an honest guy. Coyote told him, 'You know, a big chief like you shouldn't even have to go up there and kill them deer. Lend me your staff, and I'll bring one down. Just tell me how you do it.'

Wood Tick said, 'Well, don't hit more than once on the ground.' He said, 'One a day – just one. Bring it back and put it here, in that corner.'

'Okay,' Coyote said.

Coyote tried. He struck the staff on the ground. 'Gee, that's great!' Down came a deer. He gutted it out – dragged it home. This went on for a few days. One day, 'Bang! Bang!' – just kind of slipped. Down came two, but nothing happened.

Wood Tick already knew about it. Warned him, 'Coyote,' he said, 'I told you just one!'

Coyote said, 'Last day I slipped. I didn't know the stick went down again – I pretty near fall on my face trying to brace myself.'

'Okay,' Wood Tick said, 'don't let it happen again, or you're a goner!'

'That's okay, I won't let it happen again,' Coyote said, making new moccasins, making his partner new clothes, making him feel good. Wanted to gain his trust every time he went hunting. Until one day he got into his foolish mood again. 'This is foolish, crazy coming over here once a day!' he said, 'I'm going to bring home a week's supply and I won't have to walk over here every day.'

'Bang! Bang! Bang!' and down came the deer and the stick wouldn't quit bouncing. The deer just fell all over him – landed on top of him and squashed him down on the bottom, and then he jumped up and he ran because he broke the spell of the stick. The deer ran right by the camp. And all the old bones that were laying down there jumped back together, and all the skins went to their own bones, and they were all mended together, and they ran. Coyote was grabbing for one chunk here, trying to take a bite. Taking bites of deer going by, but they stampeded on by him. They were all gone. Wood Tick jumped on the last deer going by – that is when he turned into a wood tick. He jumped and landed behind the deer's ear – carried himself a ways. The wood tick is always there now.

Coyote looking around there. There were a bunch of bones over there. 'They couldn't have gone.' He looked over there and they were gone. 'Buried some over there,' he looked and they were gone. 'All my lunch – at least I'll eat that dried meat.' The dried meat was gone – everything. It all went back together and left. Coyote was taking advantage of Wood Tick's kindness and courtesy. So Coyote, because of his greed, was punished.

Coyote Visits His Daughter in the North

Told by Herb Manuel

In a lot of Coyote stories, he had a wicked character. He always wanted to be in the company of women. He did so in so many ways. Generally, he had sons, but in this event he had daughters – two daughters. One of them was married up in cold country, far north.

And he was roaming about here and he had a lump in his heart, thinking, 'Oh, my God! My daughter! It's been a year now – she must have a child!' So he thought to himself, 'Well, I'll go and make a visit.' But he had some weird thoughts in his mind. He didn't like the person that his daughter married. It was Lynx.

So he went in pursuit of his daughter. He went up. It took him days and days to get up there. When he got to where his daughter lived, he looked and thought, 'Oh, my goodness! I have a super son-in-law!' Deer hides all over, hanging on the trees. There was another pithouse. It was filled full of hides and bones. 'Gee!' he said, he hadn't eaten for days. He jumped out there and started munching on the bones – just tearing into the old hides.

And his daughter heard something out there. Her husband was out hunting and she recognized him, 'Hey, dad! What are you doing? Come on over! Get away from there! Get over here! I'll feed you something if you're hungry! Don't eat on that untanned buckskin over there! Leave the bones alone! I have some good meat over here! Come see your grandchild!' So he went down into the lodge there and spoke to his grandchild, and he was quite happy and content.

His daughter had beautiful buckskin dresses, tanned beautifully. Coyote would take bites out of her buckskin dresses no matter how much she fed him. All of her dresses were getting ruined because he was munching on her clothes.

His son-in-law came back from hunting – told him, 'Okay, let's eat,' and they'd eat. They put all the roast all around, and he had a way of doing things – shrinking them. He would shrink a whole deer so it would be just one rib. And he was sitting there and his grandson had all the roast out. He looked – nothing there. He looked – 'Oh, gosh!' he was sitting there. 'Gee, that's funny! I had roasted all the deer here – just a rib there.' Coyote by his powers he shrank the deer into one rib and he knew that he would be offered that piece.

Coyote said, 'I'm kind of a little hungry.'

'Well, you eat this rib here and I'll go out and get some more and I'll roast some more on the fire.'

'Okay,' said Coyote. So he took the rib. He took a bite out of it and put it away. That was a whole deer. He figured that would be his lunch when he left.

So he did this for many days, and his son-in-law got a little bit suspicious and left him – crawled out of there. Put Coyote to sleep down there – left him sleeping down there with what meat there was inside, and he froze him. He created ice. It was about four feet thick over the top of the pithouse for a long ways around. It was solid down in where he was. Those pithouses are about forty feet in diameter, about eight feet high.

So Coyote woke up and found the situation he was in – he couldn't move. He was frozen – stuck to the ice, stuck to the ground. The only thing he could move was his tongue. So he started licking the ice. He licked open a hole. He couldn't reach it any more, so he licked around down. Somehow he undone his arm and passed his arm up. He somehow used his fingers. He stuck them in the bottom of his tongue on top and he licked – he done that with all his fingers. Then he passed up his other arm. Pretty soon it was no good. He would keep licking, and licking, and licking – and then he used his legs. And, by golly, he just could see daylight up there now.

He was just a little short. The only thing he had left was his toe. So he passed that up. That was enough to lick a hole through the top of the ice. Now he had to pass the rest of his parts up, through the same chain. So he thought to himself, 'The first thing I got to pass up there is my eyes. So I could look around to see what's happening up there.' So his eyes went up first. He passed his eyes through the hole up top. No sooner did his eyes land up top than Raven came by – picked up his eyes – took his eyes. He got the rest of his body up there, little by little. He put himself back together. When he got himself together, he knew his eyes were gone already, so he started down from the high mountains.

He walked along. He'd run into a tree and he'd ask the tree, he'd holler up, 'What type of tree are you?'

The tree would answer, 'I am balsam.'

As the trees grew different at different heights, he knew how high he was. When the tree said he was balsam, he knew he was in high mountain country, so he kept on walking downhill, and he would ask the trees here and there when he walked into them. They'd answer – tell him what kind of tree he was in, then he'd go along. He run into a fir tree, 'I'm getting near now.' He was thirsty and he had no water. He was looking for water, so he kept going downhill. He would be going along, hitting trees, and he'd ask them, and they'd answer him back. Finally, he hit a big old pine tree at the bottom of the hill, so he went along the flat, hitting trees. Pretty soon he hit an aspen tree. Well, when he hit the aspen, he said, 'I'm getting near water.' He hit a cottonwood and said, 'Well, I'm getting closer to water.' When he hit the willows, he knew he was close to water. So he went along.

He listened – he heard the water rippling down there. 'Oh, yeah!' he had a drink of water – a good drink, and he felt better. He felt around there. There were bushes and the berries were ripe, so he munched on berries. Anything he could find he stuffed in his mouth.

He was going downstream, along the little stream, and followed it down. He figured, 'Well, I will keep following the streams – when they get bigger, I'm going to hit the big stream. That's where the people live.' That was in his mind. So after two or three streams, he hit a good-sized stream, and he ate the berries as he went along, and he got to this one little flat, and he was tired. He was sitting there – he didn't know if it was day or night. He just moved along when he wasn't tired because he couldn't see.

All of a sudden he thought he heard something. He listened again. He went down a little further and he could hear them. Young girls – there was four young girls picking berries along the stream. Coyote had a plan already. 'I have a plan. I'm going to go down there and steal the eyes off one of them girls,' he said. 'Always the youngest is the easiest,' he says. So he went along there.

They seen him. The older one said, 'Oh, that looks like Coyote!'

He said, 'I'm out here to show the people something they have never seen before. I was sent here to do that. You know that star up there?' They all looked up there – they didn't see nothing. Coyote said, 'No, you can't see it from over there. This is the only place, right here where I'm standing. See this big rock I'm standing on?' So he stood on the rock, looked up there, and said, 'See? Right from here. If you see that star, you will be lucky all your life.'

The young girls looked up, 'Ah, that's Coyote! He just wants to con you!'

Coyote said, 'No, no! Come on over and have a look!'

The young girl started running over there. She was inquisitive. Her sisters were trying to grab her, but she continued on running, 'Where is it?'

Coyote said, 'Right up there! See?'

'Ah yeah, right here!' said the young girl.

He got her behind the head – like this. 'Come right over here, close. See back here, see way up there,' he said. 'Blink two times and then open your eyes real wide.' And she done that. Coyote plucked out her eyes, and he popped them in his sockets. Coyote took off, and the little girl was howling around there, and they gave chase for a little ways. But now Coyote was doing good – he had her eyes.

These women were different birds, and the youngest one was a wren. So he had the eyes of the wren. He could see, but as he walked along he was getting hungry, and the only thing he could see was insects and berries – he couldn't see meat. His wren eyes were trained for insects and berries, so he had to live on insects and berries as he went along.

In the meantime, the women up above there were trying to find new eyeballs for their little sister. They tried every berry they picked around there. They tried some other berries, and they fixed them and put them into her eyes. They blew on them – no! They worked and worked at it. Finally there were these little red berries – the ones that grow flat on the ground there – the kinnikinnick berries. Those berries, they tried those berries in her eyes, 'My god, I can see!' So they left them on there permanent. The wren is about the size of a robin. They usually migrate through here. I see them in the spring and in the fall when they go by – their eyes are red. That was from this event, how the little sister got to see again.

Meantime, Coyote was coming back through. And the Lytton people, after they lost their ball, Raven came down and sold them Coyote's eyes to play with. So they were throwing these eyes back and forth.

Anyway, Coyote came along down the hill, somewhere way back, up above Lytton – maybe towards Lillooet somewhere. He ran across an old woman in a little hut, kind of broke down and shabby. He seen her walking around there, gathering wood. He studied her for a while. So he went over there and talked to her, 'What are you doing?'

'I just live here.'

'Why are you all alone?'

'I'm not alone. I have four young granddaughters. Our granddaughters leave me every day,' she said. 'They go for a big sport way down there at Lytton,' she said. 'They go down to watch and have fun. They come back late in the evening and I have their meal cooked.'

So he started quizzing her, 'What do you do? What do you do first when you get up?'

'I build a fire – warm up what there is to eat for them. They'd eat. I wake the oldest one up, and then she would wake the other girls up, and I would make sure they all go for their baths – and when they came back, they'd eat. As soon as they finish, away they'd go.'

Coyote asked, 'Then what did you do the rest of the day?'

'Ah, I clean the house up – make their beds. My eyes are poor, but they have a lot of berries picked over there. I go around, feel around, pick a few fresh berries. There is some meat back there some old man brought over. That's what I bring in and cook. There's plenty of fish. Sometimes we're lucky – I have a trap down there in the creek,' she said. 'I catch fish there now and then, so we change our diet. I cook whatever I can.'

Coyote said, 'What're the girls' names?'

So she named them all.

Coyote said, 'What is the oldest one called?'

She told him.

'Second oldest?' All the way down. He wanted to know all the details – what they do, what she would do for them.

At just about sunset, he clubbed the old woman and grabbed her by the nose and shook her – like that. Her bones and meat came out and he slipped the skin over himself. He got inside the old woman's skin – everything but his long nose. That gave him away – so he had to get some pitch and some feathers to fix his nose. His tail was big and long, so he tucked his tail in somewhere down there. He sat down. He did what the old woman said they'd be doing.

All the girls came home – they were talking about the event.

Then he ask them, 'What were you doing there?'

'Oh, same thing.'

'What do you mean same thing? My memory is starting to go on me.'

'Oh, you know. They were throwing Coyote's eyes back and forth, and so they went on down the line until eventually everybody got into the game somewhere down the line.'

'Oh, that sure is interesting!' he said. 'You know I sure get tired of just sitting around here! Now that you girls are going to start playing,' he said, 'take me with you.'

'Granny, you can hardly walk! How are we going to take you down there?'

'Oh,' he said. 'This might be the last event I ever see! I sure want to see you girls get in the game!' he said. 'Oh, gosh,' he said, 'sounds interesting!' They keep trying to push her back. 'No, you got to take me down there, then I'll stay over there for a few nights. Then you can bring me back when it's finished. We'll take a lunch.'

'Okay,' they finally said. 'Alright, we'll have to pack you. Got to get an earlier start.'

So they took off earlier. It was the youngest who insisted, 'Oh, yes! We must take our granny – she goes nowhere!'

So they used to have gut strips for packing, made out of deer gut. They made out a little harness. He sat there in the back. Started going, going, a ways down the road there. He fell asleep and started snoring too loud and began talking in his sleep, so the youngest throw her down.

Her sisters came and said, 'Why do you throw granny down like that?'

'Ah, she is no good!'

'Ah, you shouldn't throw her down!'

'You pack her then!'

The second youngest, same thing happened – she threw her down. And went on to the oldest one – just getting to the edge of the playing field – throw her back down on the ground there.

Anyway, they were getting a little late for the game – it had started already. People were passing the ball back and forth, back and forth. One day went by. Just the oldest girl had a chance, and they wanted to go home, but she said, 'Ah, let's camp here on the edge of the playing field. Just get me some water and I'll be alright. Bring me some lunch tomorrow.' So that they done. Another day went by – second day – third day.

On the fourth day he was really getting into it – just a-cheering like the dickens! And he said, 'Gee, I wish I was young again! If only I could just throw the Coyote eyes, just once! Oh, I would feel so much younger! I would even walk home!'

'Walk home?'

'Yeah!'

'I think we'll give her a chance at the eyes.' She asked the opponents, 'Is it alright if we let our granny throw the eyes just once?'

They talked to them, 'What harm could she do. Let her throw it.'

She limped on into the lineup over there. They passed her the eyes. Instead of throwing them, she plucked those two eyes out of there. 'I got my eyes!' he hollers. He put his eyes in and he took off – got his eyes back. He dropped those little red bird eyes, and then he could see, and he took off up this way [Douglas Lake] from Lytton.

They chased him, and when they finally caught up he caused a fog. All he had to do was use his magic and the fog would just come out like that. He done that, he done that about twice as he run. They just about caught up to him and he caused a thick fog, and he didn't know where he was and he would go up a little higher. He kept on doing that. The people gave up their chase. So he got his eyes back and he carried on into this valley to do what he does best – mischief.

Coyote and the Two Sisters

Told by Mandy Brown

A LONG TIME AGO, they said there were two girls that planned to go and pick sk'áṁats [root of the yellow avalanche lily], tatúweṅ [corms of the western spring beauty, also known as wild potatoes], mula7 [edible bulb], and some wiẏe [black tree lichen]. They had a little dog, k̲wtíx̲a7 – that's 'louse' in English. So they started going. There used to be a stump about halfway up Petáni [Botanie] road. They were going up that road. On the way up there was a stump; they say that's where Coyote used to sit long ago, and he saw all the passers-by that went through.

Coyote was sitting there at the time these two girls were going through, and he asked them, 'Where are you going?'

'Oh, we are going up to the lake. We are going to Petáni to pick some Indian potatoes,' so they kept on going. They went so far, and it was getting dark, so they had to fix up beds from fir boughs. Long time ago, they broke the branches and pushed them in and they fixed themselves a bed. Then they put sticks over them and they covered it with more fir boughs. So the girls went to sleep. They had their k̲álex̲ [digging stick] sticking outside. They had a little camp that they made themselves.

In the morning, the little sister had her k̲álex̲ sticking just outside her sleeping place, and there was something hanging on it when she woke up.

So the big sister asked her, 'Where did this come from?'

The little sister said, 'I don't know where it came from.'

So they kept on going. On the second night, they camped again and the same thing happened the next morning. The little sister had a little bundle on her digging stick again, and they looked at it, and there was some food. They didn't know who gave it to them, but they wouldn't eat it. Long time ago, they wouldn't accept anything that was given without knowing who it was from. So they didn't eat it, they just threw it away.

They kept on going, and this time when they camped the big sister said, 'This time I'm going to watch,' because her little sister got into trouble – she got pregnant on the way up. So this time, the big sister said, 'I'm going to stay awake this time and see who's been coming around visiting my little sister.' So she stayed awake and listened. Pretty soon she heard somebody coming, so she went out – it was still kind of daylight and she saw Rabbit. She was so mad at Rabbit. She thought it must have been Rabbit that got her little sister pregnant, so she got her digging stick and she threw it at Rabbit and hit him right on his nose. That's why the rabbit has a slit nose now.

They went further up and camped again, in Petáni this time. Then the big sister saw Coyote going around her little sister's camp. He was the guilty one – he was the one who got the little sister pregnant, and Rabbit got the blame.

When they got to Petáni they started digging sk'áṁats, and they were going to cook them. Sk'áṁats are long, and they have a hollow inside – if you break one, it's hollow inside. The sk'áṁats they had picked were left laying around overnight. The next day the big sister thought, 'Well, we're going to have some of our sk'áṁats to eat. She took some in, and one was a nice big sk'áṁats. She broke it in half and there was a hair in it, and she was so mad she had seen this hair – it was an evil spirit. If there's hair in there, and if you eat it, something will happen to you. But she saw it before she put it in her mouth.

Coyote just happened to be around, close by. So Coyote got the blame for that. She was so mad at Coyote, she went after him – and Coyote was so scared. The way they howl, they kind of cry. She went after Coyote, she hit him, and Coyote started crying – that's why they cry like that today. The way they cry, they howl as if they're crying up in the hills.

They dried all the sk'áṁats. They dug a hole there and they buried them until they were ready to come down because they didn't trust the coyotes or whatever animals that are out there. They might do something with the Indian potatoes, so they buried them. When they were ready to come down, they took all the Indian potatoes and they packed them down.

There's two things in this story – how the rabbit got a slit on its nose and why coyotes howl.

Why Newborn Animals Can Walk

Told by Mandy Brown

THIS STORY is about why animal babies can walk just a few minutes after they are born, and why human beings can't walk until they are about a year old.

This story took place where the rivers meet in Lytton. The human mother was on this side, and Coyote was on the other side – where that big rock is. There's a big rock across there – it's been there for years. You can see it, if you go down, look across the river. Long time ago, it used to be really cold. There was ice right across the river – I remember it.

The human mother was on this side. She was going to go across the river, but she didn't make it. She had a baby. She had her baby on this side and she didn't want her baby to walk. She wrapped up her baby and she carried it over.

While Coyote across the river, she had a child – a baby Coyote. She says, 'Oh, I'm not going to pity my baby! My baby can walk – you don't let your baby walk. I'm going to let my baby walk across the ice.' So when Coyote had her child, she started walking across on the ice and her child followed her, while the human being wrapped her child and carried it across the ice. They say that's why we don't walk until we are about a year old, whereas the animals, they walk just a few minutes after they are born.

Grizzly and the Bear Cubs

Told by Hilda Austin
Translated by Dorothy Ursaki

I'M GOING TO TELL YOU a story about Sk̲wik̲wtl'k̲wetl't. He was Bear's youngest cub – there were four of them. The female Bear took for a husband a Grizzly. They lived happily together, and then Grizzly must have got tired of Bear.

One day after waking up in the morning, Bear and Grizzly went for a walk. They stopped, and Grizzly said to his wife, 'I am going to look for lice in your head and hair.' So they looked for lice in each other's heads and hair. While looking for lice in his wife's head and hair, he bit her on the back of her head, which killed her.

Bear and Grizzly had four cubs each. The cubs were all left at their home while the couple went for their walk. The Bear cubs must have known what was going to happen. Before Bear left her cubs, she told them to make some pudding for themselves, and she told the Grizzly cubs to make some pudding for themselves also. The cubs said to their mother, 'Alright.'

So when mealtime came around, the Bear cubs made their pudding and so did the Grizzly cubs. The Bear cubs made a thick pudding while the Grizzly cubs made their pudding watery. All the Grizzly and Bear cubs ate their pudding after their meal.

The Bear cubs said, 'Now we are going to go bathing – now that we are finished our meal.' So the Bear and Grizzly cubs went bathing. They must have done something to one of the Grizzly cubs, as it died. Anyway, the Bear cubs brought the dead Grizzly cub to shore, and soon one by one the rest of the Grizzly cubs all died.

Grizzly said to his cubs before he left, 'Bake me the youngest Bear cub, and erect it on the path I use to come here.' The Grizzly thought that all the Bear cubs would die, but instead the Grizzly cubs died. The Bear cubs must have heard that this was going to happen, because they baked the youngest Grizzly cub and erected the dead body on the path Grizzly would take when coming home.

Then they ran away.

The Grizzly father, now coming home, saw the dead body of a Bear cub. It made him happy, as he did not know it was one of his cubs. He started to eat the baked carcass. When nearly finished eating, he recognized one of his cub's paws. He saw that his Grizzly cubs were all dead in bed, and so he went on the trail looking for the Bear cubs, following their footprints, chasing after them.

Grizzly came across Squirrel. They started to argue with each other. Grizzly pawed at Squirrel and then chased him. Squirrel quickly ran into a hole in the ground, but Grizzly caught him and held him there. That is how Squirrel got his white mark on his back. Grizzly left Squirrel and went on his way trailing the Bear cubs.

In the meantime, the Bear cubs were on their way too. One said, 'There's someone close behind us!' Close to the trail they saw an ant hill. They wrapped up all the ants and took them along with them. The Bear cubs came to a large tree and they all climbed it. Grizzly caught up to them.

The Bear cubs said to Grizzly, 'Lie down on your back and we will throw down our youngest brother to you!'

'Oh, Alright!' said Grizzly.

As he lay down with his back on the ground and his mouth and eyes wide open, the Bear cubs said to Grizzly, 'We are going to throw our youngest brother down to you!' Instead, they threw the ants into his mouth and eyes.

The four Bear cubs came down from the tree and ran away. Grizzly, with his eyes and ears full of ants, growled in pain.

The youngest Bear cub said, 'Oh! The Grizzly is coming – he will catch up to us!' The Bear cubs reached the river's edge, and they saw Sk̲waní7k̲wa [the name of their grandfather] across from them fixing his canoe, hammering on his canoe.

The four Bear cubs hollered over to him, 'Sk̲waní7k̲wa! Come take us across the river to your side! Grizzly will be catching up to us and will eat us up! So come for us!' So he came for the four Bear cubs in his canoe.

When the Bear cubs reached the other side of the river, they said to S<u>k</u>waní7<u>k</u>wa, 'Now make a hole in the bottom of your canoe, so when Grizzly arrives and asks you to go over the river to get him, you can tell him to sit where the hole in the boat is!'

Not long after their conversation, Grizzly arrived at the edge of the river opposite from them. Grizzly yelled over to S<u>k</u>waní7<u>k</u>wa, asking him to come across the river and get him. He also asked S<u>k</u>waní7<u>k</u>wa if he had seen the four Bear cubs arrive.

S<u>k</u>waní7<u>k</u>wa said, 'Yes, they have come and gone. I have brought them over here in my canoe.'

Grizzly answered, 'Hurry! Hurry! Come get me so I can go chasing after those four Bear cubs!'

So S<u>k</u>waní7<u>k</u>wa went across to the opposite side to get Grizzly. When getting into the canoe, S<u>k</u>waní7<u>k</u>wa told Grizzly to sit where the hole was, telling him, 'If you don't sit over the hole the water will come through into the canoe and the canoe will sink and drown us!' So Grizzly sat where the hole was. Just a little ways from the shore, Grizzly yelled aloud as he stood up. S<u>k</u>waní7<u>k</u>wa said to him, 'Don't stand up!' for he saw the water coming up into the canoe. Grizzly sat down on the hole again.

The four Bear cubs told the fish to bite Grizzly on his buttocks. So a fish bit Grizzly, and he hollered aloud, crying.

S<u>k</u>waní7<u>k</u>wa said to him, 'Don't you get off that hole – the water will get into the boat!'

So Grizzly went back to the hole and sat down. Just a short time later Grizzly started to holler again and cry in pain as the animals in the water were again biting him on his buttocks. S<u>k</u>waní7<u>k</u>wa and Grizzly landed on shore, and the water animals chewed Grizzly's body up and he died.

S<u>k</u>waní7<u>k</u>wa then went home to his grandchildren and told them, 'Your enemy has died. His guts are all gone – eaten up by the water animals.' The grandchildren were told, 'Take care when you are passing by the monster, as he usually eats anything in sight. You'll have to watch him on your way home.'

Sk̲wik̲wtl'k̲wetl't replied, saying, 'Oh, we will be passing by him, and we'll talk to him.'

The Bear cubs arrived at the monster's place. The monster was sitting on the edge of the river, where he would bite the back of the heads of peoples' wives as they passed by him. Sk̲wik̲wtl'k̲wetl't said, 'We are going to slide dirt over him.' So the brothers climbed a hill above the old monster and Sk̲wik̲wtl'k̲wetl't kicked a mound of dirt, which slid down on top of the monster. The dirt slid off the old monster, and he did not fall over but remained sitting. So Sk̲wik̲wtl'k̲wetl't again kicked the earth above the old monster but did no harm to him. He remained sitting after having two earth slides dumped over him.

Sk̲wik̲wtl'k̲wetl't said, 'I am going down by the river. When I get there I'm going to turn myself into a steelhead.' So Sk̲wik̲wtl'k̲wetl't went down to the river and turned himself into a steelhead. That's why bears can swim today.

Sk̲wik̲wtl'k̲wetl't now a steelhead, saw the enormous monster, and the monster hooked him. Sk̲wik̲wtl'k̲wetl't changed himself back to a bear, took the monster's spear, and cut the rope that was tied onto it, so the monster could not hook him. The monster had no spear, so he went home and lay down – all curled up.

So Sk̲wik̲wtl'k̲wetl't changed himself back to a steelhead and arrived at the monster's house carrying the monster's spear. Sk̲wik̲wtl'k̲wetl't entered – the monster was all curled up. The monster's wife said to him, 'Go away! The monster will kill you!'

Sk̲wik̲wtl'k̲wetl't, defying the monster's wife's orders, just laughed really loud, saying, 'I found a spear – it must belong to the monster!'

As soon as the monster heard the word 'spear,' he sat up and said, 'That must be my spear!' So Sk̲wik̲wtl'k̲wetl't gave him the spear and the monster said, 'That is my spear!' This made the monster very happy, as he couldn't do anything without his spear.

Sk̲wik̲wtl'k̲wetl't left with his older brothers. Whenever they went on trips, it was the second brother's job to pack Sk̲wik̲wtl'k̲wetl't on his back.

The oldest brother threw the youngest brother's headband into the fire, which caused the river to rise and to become a large flood. The three older brothers ran away from it. While the river was flooding, Sḵwiḵwtl'ḵwetl't remained beside the fire, lying down, keeping warm. The water got so high it went over him, covering his body. The flood water reached the top, where it could go no further. The other brothers came to a tree, which they climbed. Sḵwiḵwtl'ḵwetl't saw, with his powers, that the brother that back-packed him was the last one to climb away from the flood, which meant he would be the first one to drown. And Sḵwiḵwtl'ḵwetl't thought to himself, 'My brother will be the first to be taken away by the flood waters and be drowned.' Then the water started to recede. The brother went to Sḵwiḵwtl'ḵwetl't, where he was lying beside the open fire, keeping warm. The brothers took their younger brother and left.

Grizzly and the Black Bear Cubs

Told by Mary Williams

Translated by Mamie Henry

THIS IS ABOUT what happened when a Black Bear mated with a Grizzly, who also had a Grizzly wife. He had four children by one wife and four by the other. They came to Petáni [Botanie] Valley, where they were digging roots.

Grizzly told her husband, 'Come here. I am going to look through your hair.' While pretending to clean his hair, she chewed his head and he died.

Grizzly called her rival, Black Bear, and killed her also. She then cut off Black Bear's breasts, packed them in her basket, and went home. She arrived at the lake by her home and sat down to prepare a meal. She told her children in the morning, 'You are going to make some gruel – one a heavy kind, the other a watery kind.' The children did this.

'Now you are going to kill Black Bear's children,' their mother told them. When the children all went to sleep, Grizzly got up to see where her husband was lying. In the meantime, the children woke up and ate.

After eating, they decided to go swimming. They went down to the lake and swam. They began to hold one another underwater. All of Grizzly's children died. Black Bear's children dragged them to shore and laid them in a row on a blanket. Beside them they laid figures of rotted trees. Then they left them there.

Grizzly came along and, thinking the figures were Black Bear's cubs, devoured them. Then she realized they were only rotted wood.

As for her own children, there were some roasts propped on sticks. Grizzly took one and ate. A bird spoke to her, saying, 'You are eating your children's fingertips.' She took a look and cried – they were her children!

Black Bear's children ran until they got to a spot where they decided to create a blockage. They fixed up the brush so nothing could pass. When they were finished they started running again, but Grizzly was gaining on them.

They gathered up some ants and climbed a tree, but Grizzly caught up with them. 'Your parents are here!' she said to them. 'Come on! Come home!'

'Oh, no!' the children replied. 'We are going to stay around here – we are not coming home.'

Then they relented. 'Oh, alright! If you really want us to come home, lie flat on your back.'

Grizzly lay down and the children poured the ants on her. The ants got into every part of her. She struggled up, but couldn't walk. The children scrambled down the tree and ran and ran until they came upon Chipmunk, who started calling them names.

'Where are you going, you ugly things?' cried Chipmunk.

The children called back, 'Oh, should someone come along and scratch your back, it will remain so!'

The children ran further until they came to a place called

Ng̲wuyúym̓xw [lot 47 up Botanie Road]. Coyote popped up and commanded, 'Wait there! Wait there! I want to talk to you!'

'No, no, no!' said the youngest one. 'Don't stop! Let's go! Hurry!' They were carrying the youngest one, you know.

Coyote started calling names. 'Oh, you children are no good!' he said. 'You don't listen!'

The children called back, 'May your head be stuck out forever, you Coyote!' They ran and ran until they came to the shore, where they found Sk̲waní7k̲wa hammering his canoe.

'Sk̲waní7k̲wa! Sk̲waní7k̲wa!' they cried. 'Take us across! Take us across! Hurry! Grizzly is going to kill us!' He took the children across and let them go.

Sk̲waní7k̲wa took his canoe and bored a hole in it, then stuffed the hole. By that time, Grizzly had arrived at the shore – Sk̲waní7k̲wa returned for her. Water was leaking through the hole.

'Sit there!' he told Grizzly. 'Sit really tight or we'll drown before we get to shore!' Grizzly squatted over the hole. In the middle of the river, fishes bit out her guts. She died and was thrown into the water.

Now the children were wandering throughout the country, all the way down to Lytton, then up towards the Stein. At the mouth of the Stein, there are imprints of small footprints in a rock, opposite the church. The children wandered from the Stein to the Coast, opening the rivers on their way. That's why we are now getting fish.

That's what this story is about. That's all I remember of it.

The Four Bear Brothers

Told by Anthony Joe
Translated by Mamie Henry

THERE WERE FOUR PEOPLE, all brothers. The youngest was still small and they always carried him. The little one wore a headband of beaver.

They were on their way upriver. They passed by Lytton and went on to the slide area at Spences Bridge, where they encountered a monster. No one ever passed by this place, as the monster killed anyone who tried. All he did was fish.

The smallest and youngest of the brothers said, 'If we don't pass here, we'll die for sure. Instead of crossing, we'll climb until we get to the top of the mountain. Then I'll fix the monster. See what will happen – I'm going to curse that monster!'

They started climbing, taking turns carrying their youngest brother, but before they came to the top they were tired. 'Alright,' said the youngest brother, 'we'll start here.' He gave the earth a kick and it broke – but at daylight the monster was still standing. After the fourth time the boy kicked the earth there was nothing more they could do to kill the old man, and the brothers decided to go back down.

When they reached the bottom, they bathed. While bathing, they saw the old man still looking for salmon with a pole. The smallest and youngest of the brothers said, 'You watch and see what happens to me! I'm going to turn into a salmon! I'm going to swim out – you watch me!'

He dove in and swam around – he was a salmon, alright. He had a knife, a tiny knife, which he always wore around his waist. He emerged from the water and asked his brothers how he did. They told him that he looked like a real salmon.

'Alright now,' he said, 'I'm going to fix that old man! I'll turn into a salmon, he'll spear me, and I'll cut off his spearhead – you watch me!'

The young brother lay in the water and then swam off. He was spotted by the old man, the monster, who moved quickly and alertly and speared him. The fish fought and went far out from shore, but the monster pulled until he got him close. The monster was going to club the salmon when the fish pulled on the line, snapped his eyes at the club, and swam out again and fought the line.

The fourth time he snapped his eyes, he cut the line. By that time he was far out in the river, swimming upstream and out of sight. The old man decided to go home – he raised his pole and found there was no spearhead.

The youngest brother reached his brothers and said to them, 'Look! This is what I was speared with!' The spearhead glowed like gold. He cut off the line and said to his brothers, 'Now, we shall go and see.'

They came to the old man's house. He was huddled and his wife was sitting. She exclaimed, 'I suppose you are just travelling around! How did you get here?'

'Oh, grandmother!' they said, 'We were just looking over the country. On our way, we kept fixing the land here and there and moving on. Then we decided to come and see you.'

'Oh, oh – very nice!' said the old woman. 'Take a seat.'

'We were bathing over there and found a fish,' the brothers told her. 'It was a huge spring salmon. We ate and ate until we were full, then we left. This thing was stuck in the fish. We wonder what it is!'

The monster sat up suddenly. 'Give it here, dear! Give it here, dear! I'm going to look at it!' he said to his wife.

'Here it is,' said the brothers.

'That's my spear, my dears! Thank you!' said the old man.

'We've finished all the fish – a huge salmon came along and broke my line!' Of course, all along, it was the youngest brother who did it.

'Make something for your grandchildren!' the monster said to his wife. 'Make something to eat!'

In a short while, the youngest boy finished his food and cleaned out his dish. Four scoops and he was full. The others ate and finished. The old woman took her basket, turned it over, and laid it down.

'Thank you, we are on our way now,' the brothers said. They travelled until they were tired, then stopped and made a fire for their little brother. The oldest brother took his little brother's headband and threw it in the fire. The river began to rise. They fled to the top of the rock and climbed higher, but still they were going to die.

The next-to-youngest brother spoke up. 'I'm going to die!' he mourned.

The river began to go down. The brothers fled down with the water, but they could not catch up to it. The water became the way the river runs now. The boys were saved, and, carrying their little brother, they fixed up the country all over again.

The old people later told this story of how the brothers fixed up the country to be as it presently is. Now you can see those brothers in the stars. This is a long story, but that's where those people are now – the four brothers are in the stars. That's the story of the old folks.

Transformers

Told by Louie Phillips

WELL, UP HERE IN SHAW SPRINGS, you go a mile up further – landslide there [this place is known as Zexzéx or Mudslide]. Transformer and his brothers were going up that way and Coyote was spearing fish across the river between them two little tunnels. You can see a little hollow there yet – between the tunnels where Senk'iy̓áp [Coyote] was lying against a bluff with his spear. Steelhead go through, he would spear them out, and these transformers seen him there.

There's three brothers, and they tell each other, 'We're going to go up.' That land still comes down once in a while. They get up on top, Senk'iy̓áp would hold his spear and they would kick the dirt from way up top – it slides down. Buried him up and the river washed the dirt away – dirt’s all gone. ‘Goddamn! Senk’iy̓áp’s still holding his spear!’ They can’t do nothing with him.

So they come down to the river and the oldest one is thinking how he’s going to catch Senk’iy̓áp. He always uses his little brother for something. He says, ‘I am going to make a bridge out of you. We’re going to go over – steal his spearhead.’ So he just grabbed his little brother and shook him across the river and there’s a bridge – a bridge across – the little brother was a bridge! They go over, get there, and he tell his little brother, ‘Now we’re going to take the bridge off, make tsúg̱wlha7 [steelhead] out of you. Your fur is going to change into flints, like arrowheads – all your fur. Going to be steelhead. You go up the river, he’s going to spear you, and you’re going to fight around. You cut the hemp that’s attached to the spear and come back.’

So his brother went up. Senk’iy̓áp sees a big tsúg̱wlha7 coming up and he spears him. He pull around a little bit – the little brother took the spearhead off. Senk’iy̓áp went back. He’s got a den up there on a hillside, where he lives. His wife is up there.

So the boys went up – make lots of wood for the old woman. Pack some water – got to pack water from the river just so Senk’iy̓áp wouldn’t kill them. Going to make something good that he’d like so he wouldn’t kill them – they pack water and they make lots of wood.

He got there and his wife asked him, ‘How did you make out?’

‘Got a big steelhead!’ he said, ‘He fight – he break the hemp from my spearhead! He took my spear!’ They were talking there for a while.

The boys said, ‘There was a steelhead lying on the beach. We picked him up, looked at him. He’s got a spearhead in him.’

He looked at it. ‘Oh!’ he says, ‘Thank you! Thank you! That’s my spearhead that steelhead took away from me!’ And he was happy – he didn’t harm the boys. But the old woman was scared, she thought he was going to do something wrong to those boys because he’s a mean old devil. So the boys left.

Transformers

Told by Herb Manuel

DURING THE TIME that Coyote was transforming he brought the salmon up from the Coast and then he veered off and went north up the Fraser River and up the Thompson River – and he went through the Shuswaps and then he went across the border and brought the salmon up the Columbia River. He done that river all the way up to the Rockies. He led the fish over there as far as they can go – different species of fishes, as he went along. And he transformed different places as he went by.

Like the Columbia, much the same story of the Nlha7kápmx, where the salmon came this way. But when he was bringing the salmon towards Okanagan he stopped off at Okanagan Falls and he seen some women swimming in the river down there. He asked them, 'You women want the salmon up your country?' These women were from the Similkameen area.

'Ah, Coyote!' they said, 'we don't want no salmon! We're people that eat the muscle part of the back behind the horns of the mountain sheep. That's what our men get us for a delicacy here.'

Coyote said, 'Alright, just for that you are going to wear out many moccasins before you see the salmon.'

But anyways, during this time, there were four brothers who done some transforming. They came straight up the Fraser River. They just stopped at different places. And right here at Nicola Lake, it's the only place where they did some transformations here.

There were two cannibals there and the trail went down the middle, straight down there, right where the lakes narrow down there. Right there on the other side up the mountain, just above Monck Park [at Nicola Lake] that man lived over there. His name was Stemálst, and on this side S<u>x</u>witl'áts'ank – the Nlha7kápmx name for mountain goat. So that was his sister, the mountain goat – but she was a beautiful female.

So whenever people travelled along, especially men, she would lure them into his house, which after that was always known as nx̱a7x̱a7átkwu – sacred waters [Nicola Lake]. Before that lake was formed, there was just a flat down there. He had a door on this side, and, right under the road where the sharp corners are – there was another door. She would invite them in for something to eat and her brother would kill them and eat them. The whole outside was a pile of bones.

The Transformers came by from the Coast and they were suspicious of this thing, and they knew in their minds what was happening there. The youngest had not tested his powers yet. So the youngest of the four wanted to test his powers before they went back to the Coast on their last mission. So he went ahead to be grabbed by Stemálst. So he was invited in by Stemálst's sister and after they had a meal Stemálst killed him and ate him up and threw his bones out. That's when his brothers transformed Stemálst into a stone mountain over there, and his sister – the same – on this side.

And Stemálst had two dogs on the other side – they wouldn't let the traffic go by. When the people were coming, these dogs would block the passage. The mountains were so steep they couldn't go by any other way. They would have to go way far around. The only way he would call his dogs back was if they came in to eat. One was a grizzly bear and one was a rattlesnake.

So when they were transformed and petrified – the sister being on the south side and the brother being on the north side – their dogs were also transformed. And the Transformers built a lake between them, because the man was fooling around with his sister. That's what the Transformers didn't like – that's why they put the lake between them. The dogs were transformed into some type of serpent that stayed under the water. It had the body of a snake and the head of a grizzly.

The waters right between those two mountains [Nicola Lake] were always sacred to the people. They won't bathe around there. If they needed high powers in medicine, they came. It's the only time they dared to go there – but slowly, while talking to the mountain. They would sleep on the mountain for powers, but there is still fear. People my age, who know the language, still fear that the Nx̱a7x̱a7átkwu is there. X̱a7x̱á7 is kind of a spooky, scary, unpredictable thing.

Anyway, transformation was made by beings other than Coyote – Coyote did most of the other things around.

Transformer Footprints

Told by Louie Phillips

IN STEIN FLAT, the Transformer came through there and he stepped on a granite rock on the old Indian trail – just looked like a ditch. The Transformer stepped on the granite rock – looks like, oh, about seven-year-old, eight-year-old kid's foot. The footprint sank into the granite about a sixteenth of an inch. One is a little ways behind the old Stein church, and the other footprint is halfways down the dry flat. Must have been a tall person.

See, them days there was no bridge, and they go down Stein flat and go down the mouth of Stein Creek. Well, Stein River flattened out wide and you can walk – maybe water up to your waist. And I guess he was going down there to cross, and the crazy monkey should have made a bridge that time when he was coming through.

Up from Stein you go up behind Npatús [narrow valley on the north side of the Stein River], and there's a little horse trail. I don't know what I was doing up there. I was going along there – there's a black bedrock, real black, sticking out there and I see a goat track sunk into a rock. I bet you that rock was mud. And lots of sáma7 [White people] ask me about it. I tell them, 'I can't walk up there. I can tell you about it, what I seen, but I can't walk up there to show. I have to have crutches – wheelchair.'

Them people born, raised there – they can't even find them

Transformer tracks. Right there at Stein, right there in the little flat. From the little church, about 120 yards behind the little church, you see one footprint there and you go way down. Like a road going to the cemetery, there's one lone pine tree – you get to that pine and from that pine tree look north-west, and you run into the other footprint. And them guys live there and they got good ornaments there. Well, my father was raised there and he showed it to me. You can't miss it, that old trail. There are so many Indians here, that trail is looking like a ditch. And on the side – that granite rock with the footprint on it. Yeah, there's lots of things around here, if you can find them.

How Chipmunk Got His Stripes

Told by Mandy Brown

THIS IS HOW Chipmunk got the stripes on his back.

They say long ago there was a chipmunk living under a big rock. One time he was sitting outside and Bear was going by. He started teasing Bear, 'Oh, you big clumsy old thing!' and 'You can't even get around as good as I can!' Bear got mad and went after Chipmunk. Chipmunk went back in his hole and Bear couldn't catch him. Chipmunk came out again and started teasing Bear again. Bear went after him, but couldn't catch him and missed Chipmunk again. But the third time Bear got Chipmunk on his back and kind of scratched him. They say that's how Chipmunk got the little stripes on his back.

Screech Owl

Told by Mandy Brown
Translated by Dorothy Ursaki

LONG AGO, people would play lhkw̓úsa7ma [a game involving throwing an object into the air and piercing it with a dart] and bake in their pithouses.

One day, children were playing inside a pithouse and accidentally started a fire. The people had to get out by climbing a ladder, because there are no doors in pithouses. They all climbed up the ladder, but Screech Owl missed a step and fell to the bottom of the ladder. The others trampled on him. When they finally got off him, one of his friends got him up and out of the pithouse. That is why Screech Owl has a flattened face.

Raven

Told by Mandy Brown
Translated by Dorothy Ursaki

MANY YEARS AGO, Raven stole some sts'uwén [dried salmon]. While eating it, he got a fish bone stuck in his throat. One of his friends jumped on his throat to get rid of the fish bone, and that is why Raven caws the way he does.

The Boy Who Was Abandoned

Told by Mary Williams
Translated by Mamie Henry

THIS STORY HAPPENED right here in Lytton – it's about a poor boy that everyone disliked. Everyone spoke together and decided to get rid of him.

'Take him to Npuypíychen' [a creek north of Lytton], they decided. 'Plaster his eyes with pitch, urinate on him, spit on him, blow snot on him. By the time he gets his eyes clean we'll be far away, climbing to Petáni.'

While some of the people were plastering the boy's eyes, the others packed and bundled everything and left for Petáni. His grandmother disagreed, and she was left behind too. They put an old basket over her and left her in the pithouse – they left a few dried salmon for her in one room.

All alone, the boy was going along wailing, 'hi7!' [wailing sound]. Everything he could obtain, such as dried pine needles and dried grass, he put on his head. Going along with no one around, he came to a huge overturned old basket. 'What is this basket doing here?' he wondered. He kicked it over, and his grandmother was under it.

'Stop it, dear! Stop it!' she hollered. 'I don't know why the people have done this to us, but they have left us behind!' The old woman still had a little spark in her bosom, which she could blow on and burn to make something to eat. She gave it to the boy and told him to take it and fix it to make it burn.

'The people may have left us some food,' she told the boy. 'Look around the other buildings.' The boy searched through all the houses. He found a few things, brought them in, and fixed something to eat.

After the two had eaten, the old woman said to the boy, 'Sleep now, dear – sleep. In the morning you're going to go wash your face in the spring. That water is really wonderful – it is from the Creator. He gave it to us.'

First thing the next morning, his grandmother woke the boy and told him to go to the spring and wash his face. When he returned he made bows and arrows and other weapons, which he gave to his grandmother. She examined them and told the boy that they were good.

'Now I can go and shoot mice, magpies, rats, and anything else I can find,' said the boy. 'I'll bring them to you and you can fix them for me.' This the boy did. He shot many little animals and brought them to his grandmother. She skinned them for him, sewed a patchwork, and made several lovely blankets. The boy took them to hang outside.

'You'd better not, dear,' the grandmother warned. 'Sun is not very kind – he will kill you. That's not good – I'm afraid!'

'No,' the boy replied, 'don't be afraid. I'm going to go and hang up my blankets.' He crawled out from the pithouse, hung up the blankets, and sat around.

A short time later a flashing light in the form of a man appeared before him. This was Sun. 'My friend, I very much admire your blankets,' he said to the boy. 'Here, I brought you a rifle and this is something to put into it – gunpowder. You are going to give me your blankets,' he continued. 'I'm going to gather all the deer into one ravine and that's where you will go hunting. The people who have disowned you will go hungry – they will be so hungry they will be pitiful.'

The boy was reluctant to give away his blankets because they were decorated with bluejays and other pretty things, but finally he sold them. Sun rose up like a flash of fire reaching into the sky.

The boy gladly told the news to his grandmother. 'My friend brought me a rifle. Feel it,' he said.

The grandmother felt the rifle and asked, 'What will you do with this? You don't know how to use it.'

'I know how,' the boy replied. 'My friend showed me. He took the blankets, just as I told you. He also told me where to shoot deer.'

'Oh well, whatever ...' said his grandmother.

Early the next morning, the boy again washed at the spring and then left to hunt. He came home with a large number of deer. 'I won't be able to fix these for you,' his grandmother told him, 'not any more.'

'I'll fix them myself,' the boy said. 'I know how – I was taught how to fix skins.' He began cutting up the meat and hanging it to dry. 'Feel it,' he told his grandmother.

'Oh, my dear, you did well!' said his grandmother. 'Now we'll eat it.'

The boy's parents arrived home and found their son still alive and now a grown man. They visited their son at his house, but he would not give his people anything. The father wept, hungry for all that meat, while his son felt wonderful at heart.

You see now how Sun turned himself into a man and came to earth. The grandmother was very proud of the boy.

Sore Man

Told by Mabel Joe
Translated by Dorothy Ursaki

ONCE THERE WAS A STORY, long ago, about a boy who cried and cried and his parents could not stop him. He would not go to sleep, so one of the boy's parents said, 'We'll call Owl so he can take you away! Owl will take you away!'

The people all went to sleep except the grandmother, who called Owl. During the night the grandmother heard someone come – it must have been Owl. The boy was crying, and Owl put him into a large basket and took him away. The people woke up and did not hear the boy crying any more. They noticed the boy was taken away by Owl.

Owl kept the boy for quite a while. He fed the boy food, including snakes, mice, groundhogs, and squirrels. The boy ate the food he was given, as he was hungry.

The boy stayed with Owl until he grew up and knew how to hunt. He hunted deer. One day, while hunting, he noticed smoke coming from a short distance away. He thought to himself, 'There must be people living where the smoke is coming from.' So he went there and he met some elderly people and their children.

The boy, now a grown man, would go hunting and would give the elderly people and their families some of the game he caught.

Then, one day, Crow arrived. The young man said to Crow, 'You go and look for my salmon I have dried – it is close by – and you get me some small baked pies for my parents.'

Crow said to the young man, 'Alright, I know the place where your parents are,' and left.

The young man remained with the elderly people, where he hunted and supplied them with plenty of venison. This made the elderly people very happy.

Sometimes, the young man would go home to Owl; then, the young man would leave Owl and go back to the elderly people. He did this for quite a while.

Then he said, 'I am going to look for my parents.' Where the Crow disappeared, that was where he was going to look for his parents. The elderly people prepared something for him. The young man left to look for his parents; at the same time, his parents went looking for him. So his parents were looking for him and he was looking for them.

Before he got to a bunch of houses where he was going to look for his parents, he stopped to have a sweatbath in a sweathouse – he always had sweatbaths. His parents found him and they were going to take him home, but on the way home the young man saw a sweathouse. He stopped and said to his parents, 'I'm not going home with you, I'm going to stay and have a sweatbath.' So they all stayed at the sweathouse while the young man had his sweatbath. His parents were going to take him home, but he changed himself into a mass of sores. He looked terrible. His whole body was covered with sores, including his whole face – all just burned. So his parents left him there at the sweathouse. They did not bring him home because he had changed himself into a man of sores.

On their way home, people asked the parents, 'Where is your son?'

The couple answered, 'Our son had a sweatbath and turned himself into a mass of sores, so we left him there.' The parents then went on their way home.

They came across a woman, a tall woman, who was looking for a husband. It was understood that many men wanted her for a wife, but she refused them all. All the animals also wanted her for a wife, but she also refused all of them. The parents thought, 'She doesn't want anybody here – maybe she wants the sore man!' So they said to the tall woman looking for a husband, 'You should have the sore man for your husband.'

The tall woman answered, 'Oh, alright! I'll have the sore man for my husband!' So they brought her to the sore man. When she arrived where the sore man was, he was just about to have a sweatbath. He took off his sores – his outer body – which were a terrible sight. After the outer body was off, the inner body was very nice – and the tall woman was a very nice-looking woman.

Whenever the man was going anywhere he would put his sore body on. He did this for a long time and people all knew him as the Sore Man.

One day, the Sore Man's wife must have burned his sore clothes, so that was the end of the Sore Man. The man was back to himself and was a very nice-looking man. This is the end of the Sore Man story.

I don't know if this is the correct story of the Sore Man. Anyway, it's pretty close.

Man and Owl

Told by Mabel Joe
Translated by Dorothy Ursaki

THIS STORY is about a man and Owl. This man is in camp doing things. The fire beside him was just about out, and he was busy keeping the fire going and fixing the shells for his gun. The elders were all asleep as they lay by the fireside. One of the elders said to the man, 'You go to sleep. Why sit on the chair?'

The man did not heed the order. He just remained in the chair by the fire, thinking. While sitting in his chair, the man heard Owl whooing. Owl said, 'Whoo! Whoo! Dead! Dead!' Owl kept saying, 'Whoo! Whoo! Dead! Dead!'

The man said to Owl, 'Why wasn't it me that died? Let me be the next to die!'

The elders said to him, 'Why did you say that to Owl? That Owl has powers! I guess he was telling you that someone has died or will die now. Because you said that to him, *you* are going to die!'

The man just laughed at what the elders said to him – he didn't believe them.

Owl again repeated his talk, saying, 'Whoo! Whoo! Dead! Dead!'

The man answered him, saying, 'Oh! Let me be the one to die!' Then the man must have gone to sleep. And he never woke up the next day – he died that day. He never took heed of the elders' scolding. He shouldn't have said what he said to Owl – now he's dead.

Owls have powers. Whenever you hear them talking, take notice! They are serious – not fooling! So take their talking seriously!

Dog Travels to the Sun

Told by Mabel Joe
Translated by Dorothy Ursaki

THIS STORY tells of a couple – a man and woman.

The wife said, 'I am going to have four children – one with a sun imprinted on its forehead, another with a star, another with a moon, and the fourth with lightning. I'm going to light up their foreheads.' Time went by and the woman became pregnant.

It was time for the woman to give birth – she was in labour. So her husband called in an old woman from next door to be the midwife. The child was born, and the midwife opened a piece of flooring, threw the child into the hole, and picked up a cat in its place. The midwife threw the cat to the woman and said to her, 'Here is your baby!'

The woman looked at the cat and said, 'I wanted a child, not a cat!' Anyway, the woman kept the cat as her offspring.

The woman's husband came home from work and said, 'Where is my child?'

The midwife said to him, 'There is your child!'

The couple kept their cat child. Again the woman was pregnant, and when she was in labour they again called their neighbour, the midwife, to attend her. The husband was away at work again when the child was born. The midwife threw the newborn down into an opening in the floor. That's the second child the midwife threw down under the floor. This time she threw a frog to the woman and told her, 'Here is your newborn!'

The woman said, 'I'm having offspring that I had never planned on having – not one is human – both are animals!' The woman took care of her cat and frog offspring.

The husband came and said, 'Where is my child?' They handed him the frog. They brought up their cat and frog offspring.

Again the woman was pregnant, and when she was in labour the midwife was called in to attend to her. The offspring was born and the midwife again threw the child down into an opening in the floor. So when the woman asked to see her newborn child, the midwife threw a pup to her, saying, 'Here's your newborn!'

The woman was again saddened, saying, 'All my offspring are not human! I wonder what my husband is going to say to me when he arrives!' The father came home and asked for his newborn child. His wife said, 'Here's your offspring!'

He said, 'Let me look at it.' He saw it was a pup and he was saddened, but he took it in good faith. The midwife had gone home. Anyway, the couple took care of the pup – brought it up.

Later on the woman got pregnant again – that would be her fourth pregnancy. Again when the baby was due, the midwife was called in by the husband to assist his wife. Again a child was born. The midwife threw the newborn child under the floor and handed the woman a tiny snake instead of her child. The snake was a very small newborn. The man came home from work and asked, 'Where is my child?'

They said to him, 'Here is your child!' The man was saddened when he saw the snake.

The man picked up his wife and threw her into the pigsty with the pigs.

The midwife, who was jealous of the child-bearing woman, had a young daughter of her own. She wanted the child-bearing woman's husband to marry her daughter. That's why she did this – exchanging the children for animals. So the midwife's daughter took the man for her husband, and the child-bearing woman was now in the pigsty with the pigs. She ate the food the pigs were fed. She led a miserable life in the pigsty, while the midwife's daughter lived happily with her new husband.

The daughter had a large dog. Now every time the daughter and her mother hung their laundry on the clothesline to dry, the clothes would disappear. Dog would come along and just take the laundry away and hide it – he was very powerful. The daughter would get after Dog over the clothes disappearing from the clothesline.

The babies that were all thrown under the flooring had died, but Dog had brought them up, so they now lived.

Dog said, 'I am going to see Sun because he is powerful.' Before he left, he saw that the children were alright under the house.

Dog left, looking for some medicine on his way to Sun. Dog, on his way to Sun, passed a dying tree beside his trail. Tree was just about dried up, and it said to Dog, 'Where are you going?'

Dog said, 'I am going to look for some medicine.'

Tree said, 'Look for some medicine for me too. From wherever you find some, bring me some, so I can get better. You can see I am in poor shape – I am drying up.'

Dog said, 'Oh, alright,' and went on his way.

Dog, on his way, saw a lake that had dried up. Lake asked Dog, 'Where are you going?'

Dog answered, 'I am going to Sun – I am looking for some medicine.'

Lake said, 'So you are looking for medicine. I am needing medicine too – as you can see, I have dried up.'

Dog said, 'Alright,' and went on his way.

On his way, Dog saw a cottonwood tree. Cottonwood Tree asked Dog, 'Where are you going?'

Dog answered, 'I am looking for some medicine.'

Cottonwood Tree said to Dog, 'Bring me some medicine too – as you can see, I am in poor shape.'

Dog went on his way and soon came across a bush. Bush asked him, 'Where are you going?'

Dog answered, 'I am going to Sun, looking for some medicine.'

Bush said to Dog, 'Oh, so you are looking for medicine. Well, bring me some medicine too.'

So Dog left there, on his way, and soon came across a creek that was dried up. Creek asked Dog, 'Where are you going?'

Dog answered, 'I am going to Sun, looking for some medicine.'

Creek said to Dog, 'Oh, bring me some medicine too – as you see, I am in poor condition – I am dried up.'

Dog said, 'Alright, I will bring you some medicine,' and he left the dried up creek.

Finally, he arrived at his intended place. On his journey, he told everyone he came across that he was looking for medicine. 'I'm looking for medicine,' he had said to them all. His intention was to administer medicine to the children he left behind.

Dog arrived at Sun's house. Sun was not home, but there was an elderly person there in his house. When Dog entered Sun's house, the elderly person said to him, 'Nobody ever enters this house, and yet you have entered it. This place is very powerful. Your friend is not home – he will kill you when he arrives. Nobody comes in here.'

Dog said, 'Oh, but I want to see Sun, my friend.'

The elderly person said, 'Nobody comes in here, but you can wait for him.'

So Dog waited until Sun came. Sun had set and had come home – that's why the sun comes home evenings. When Sun came home he saw Dog. He did not harm Dog, but said to him, 'Why did you come here? Nobody comes here.'

Dog answered, 'Yes, I came here because I have a problem. Four children are really hurt, that is why I am here looking for medicine – I have come to you looking for medicine. I am going to administer medicine to cure the four children so they will become healthy. These four children were beaten by an elderly woman. The children's poor mother has been put into a pigsty with the pigs.'

Sun said to Dog, 'You are to go back to where the children are and you are to lick, with your tongue, their mouths – over and over. And then lick their whole bodies. I am not giving you any medicine, but licking their bodies with your tongue will be the only medicine. And put a band around their heads – you are to give the children a good cleaning.'

Dog replied, 'Alright, I will do that to the children.'

Sun said, 'Don't you forget what you have to do to the children to bring them back to life!'

Dog said, 'Alright, I'll do that.' And he said to Sun, 'On my way here to see you, I came across Tree, Lake, Cottonwood Tree, Bush, and Creek, who also want medicine to make them better.'

Sun said, 'I am not giving you medicine for them – they sleep until noon. They sleep too long – that's why they are sick.'

Dog said, 'So you are not giving them any medicine then?'

Sun answered, 'No, I'm not giving them any medicine, but you tell them all that they are to wake up early in the morning before I rise – before I leave my house. Doing this, they will get better. Tree, Cottonwood Tree, Bush, Lake, and Creek will thrive.'

So Dog left Sun's house to go back home. On his way home he delivered Sun's message to Tree, Cottonwood Tree, Bush, Lake, and Creek – if they would rise early in the mornings before Sun leaves his house each day they would get their health back. Tree, Cottonwood Tree, Bush, Lake, and Creek were all given this message from Sun.

Dog arrived back at his abode, where he had left the children, and with his tongue, he licked their four bodies, including their mouths, and the children all came alive. Dog put a band around their heads, and the children all grew.

There was a gathering of people and there were races going on. There were lots of people, and they sat outside watching the amusements.

The clothes were missing again from the clothesline – Dog had taken the clothes to put on the children.

The gathering of the people was still on, and in its midst was Dog. The man was happy to see Dog, and said, 'I am happy to see Dog. I have missed him for a long time – he has come.' Dog was also happy to see the man.

Dog left the man and, not long after, came back with the children. The children wore head bandages so it wouldn't be too bright for them. Dog went to his master [the man] with the four children standing close by. The man lifted the bandages off the first child's head and, lo and behold, there was a large star – it was very bright, and it shone all around. The man also lifted the head bandages off all the other children, and on their unbandaged heads they also had bright lights. The man was saddened.

He took Dog and the four children, with the midwife and the man's new wife sitting close by. The man stood up at the large gathering of people watching the amusements, some of whom were important people, and he said, 'Go get my wife from the pigsty – bathe her and clean her up. My children have brought Dog.' The people were glad to hear this order from the man, while the midwife and her daughter were speechless.

The people brought the wife from the pigsty. She came from the pigsty and saw her children – Moon, Star, Sun, and Lightning. She took them all.

Then the man took his second wife and her mother and put both of them on wild horses. He hired someone to tie the women securely onto the wild horses, who ran – wildly bucking.

The man was very happy to have his four children, Dog, and his wife with him again. He took good care of them all to the end. I guess the old midwife and her daughter must have died.

This is what happens today – some elders get jealous of couples living happily together and they will do anything to foil their happiness. They want their own children to take over that happiness – this is what happens in the world.

The Country Divided

Told by Annie York
Translated by Mamie Henry

THIS STORY occurred when the world was divided. At that time, a man and a woman lived with their child at Quilchena. The man died, so the woman raised the child by herself and taught him the things that he would have been taught by his father. She instructed the boy how to hunt rabbits and birds for their food.

When the boy grew older, his mother told him that they had no relatives, friends, or neighbours living nearby, so he would have to travel a long way to find a woman to become his mate. Before he left, she made him some new moccasins, snowshoes, and a fine bow for hunting. Every morning the young man bathed and sweated as his mother instructed him.

One day, while the young man was out hunting, he heard a song – a beautiful song being sung by a woman. He hid behind a tree and watched. Soon, a group of women came into the clearing, removed their clothing, and knelt down to pray. Each of the women had wings like a swan and beautiful hair. They plunged into the water. After the four women swam around in the water, they dressed and flew away into the sky.

The young man didn't say a word about what he saw. 'You certainly took a long time to come home today,' his mother said to him.

'I was lazy this morning and didn't wake up in time to have a sweatbath,' he explained.

The next day and the following day he saw these four women. Soon his mother began to wonder what he was doing out in the woods, so she said to him, 'I think it is time for you to leave and find yourself a wife and have a family. Although we are very poor, it is the proper thing for you to do.'

The next day, the young man again watched the swan-like women, and as they flew into the air, he grabbed the youngest woman's clothes. 'I have been watching you,' said the young man. 'I want you to be my wife.' She cried and cried, but when he began to plead with her, the young woman consented to go with him. He wrapped her in a deerskin cape, picked up her instrument, and carried her to his mother's house.

As the young man's mother tried to pacify the tearful young woman with the beautiful hair, she asked her son where he had found her.

The young man said, 'I have been watching her for a very long time.' While the young woman was being dressed by her mother-in-law-to-be, the young man buried her clothes and wings. 'She will leave me if she gets her clothes and wings,' said the young man to himself.

The old woman and the young woman ate and talked together. 'Where did you come from?' asked the old woman.

'My people used to live here before the world was divided. We were sent into the upper world, but once in a while we like to visit this land,' answered the beautiful young woman.

'I am very happy that you are going to stay here with us, for my son is very lonely and needs someone to talk with,' said the old woman.

The young woman was pleased when she became pregnant. But, as time went by, she became more lonely and passed the days crying. 'Would you give me my clothes, my wings, and my instrument and I will pray for you?' she begged her mother-in-law. The young man was not around, so the old woman agreed. When the beautiful young woman began to pray, the old woman became hypnotized by her song and she escaped into the air.

The young man was very angry when he returned home and found that his wife had left. 'I gave her clothes and wings to her and she flew away,' explained the mother.

'Mother, I have to leave you now! I had a dream and in that dream I was told how to travel. First, I take some skins and blow them up into a canoe shape – then I whip it all over before I get in. By doing this, I will be able to catch up to my wife.' He gathered some food and some clothing and then left in his canoe.

Soon he ran into some people who were all kneeling down praying. He got out of his canoe and prayed with them. When they had finished saying their prayers, he asked them if they had seen a young woman. 'Yes, we saw a woman go by here a long time ago – she is the one you are looking for.' They then told him that his son had been born. After he had thanked the people, they said goodbye, and the young man got in his flying canoe and left.

As he was travelling he came to a very rough place, so he got out of his canoe and took a rest. An old man approached him and asked, 'Grandson, are you travelling?'

'Yes, I am trying to find my wife,' he replied. The old man insisted that the young man stay overnight. Since he was tired, he agreed.

In the morning, the old man gave him a walking cane to take with him to another land. 'You will see lots of people in this new land,' said the old man. 'The ground will be muddy and if you are not strong enough, you will sink into the mud. My cane will help you.'

The following morning, the young man jumped into his flying canoe and left for the upper world. Before getting out of his canoe onto the muddy ground, he stuck his cane into the mud and said a prayer. After he did this, he glided along without difficulty until he came to a number of houses where there were lots of people. Everything was clean. 'Have you seen a young woman go by here?' he asked some children.

'Yes,' replied the children, 'she lives in that small house.'

Bringing his canoe to a stop, the young man peered down the entrance-way of his wife's pithouse. A tear rolled down his cheek and dropped onto the tiny face of his young son. 'Oh, it must be raining!' thought the young woman; but when she looked up, she realized that her husband had found her. She called to him and told him to enter.

There were many people in the pithouse. Some of the people were making baskets, others were sewing buckskin, and a few were weaving swan feathers into blankets. As the young man approached the group of old people, they asked him to kneel down while they said a prayer for him, and then they gave him his son. The young man was pleased and clutched his baby boy.

'We are happy that you come to take your son, as the world that we are living in will soon come to an end. There will be no more people here until once again the Creator brings them to life. We will give you some food and then you must go back to your world.' The young man listened carefully to the distressing news. A few days later, he, his wife, and their child left for his home. The young woman took her musical instrument with her, and her people warned her never to return again. The women of the village cried, sang, and played their instruments – and the young man and woman left.

They flew through the air until they came to the place where people were shooting at each other. 'Don't look at the war, for if you do, we will never get home,' warned the young man. Not long after, they landed at their home. As the man helped his wife and child out of the canoe, his mother came out of her house to greet them. 'Here is your grandson!' he told his mother. The old woman was overjoyed.

They sat and ate a feast that the woman had prepared for them, and then the young woman brought her clothes from the canoe and hung them in the house. 'I'll never leave this world again,' she told her mother-in-law.

Whenever the young woman became lonely for her people, she took out her musical instrument and played the most beautiful tunes. The baby boy grew older, but he cried for days and days.

Then, one day, a stranger appeared and said to the woman, 'From this day forth, men will die and leave the earth when their time comes. People will be separated from their friends and family – there is a way prepared for them.' The stranger said to them, 'You have lots of friends on this earth. One day, they will come from across the ocean in ships to see you.'

The young man grew and began to train for his manhood.

A foreigner arrived at the home of the young boy and told him that he and his friends were travelling. As they were hungry, the boy's mother and father gave the people some of the dried meat that they had put away and agreed to show them the hunting grounds. 'You must never prepare your food on the seventh day – you must just pray until sunset,' the man told them.

'Your wife is very beautiful,' said the strangers.

'Yes,' answered the man. 'My wife comes from another world, but she cannot go back there again. The Creator has fixed her world so that everyone has fallen asleep – although one day, the Creator will wake them up and we will see them on this earth.'

The man took the people to the hunting grounds and allowed them each to shoot four deer, which they dried. The following day, the woman called all of the people together and said to them, 'One day, people will arrive here in large ships. These people will be different from us, but we will have to learn to live together. To be able to do this, we must learn to plant food in the ground.'

The woman and her husband lived to an old age and then died. Their son, who was now a man, married a woman and had many children. The woman warned her children to find their mates in other parts of the world and to bring them home. Eventually, there were many people living where once only the young man had lived.

Long after, the White people came to this land. They were different from the original inhabitants, as they spoke a different language, ate different food, and had different customs. This is what the old woman had told the people. She had known that people in ships would arrive and teach her people how to write so that they could all communicate with each other.

Grandfather and Grandson Work for Gold and Silver

Told by Tom George
Translated by Dorothy Ursaki

I AM GOING TO TELL stories that my grandfather told me. This story is about a grandfather and his grandson. The grandson says to his grandfather, 'Let's go look for a job for us.'

The grandfather tells his grandson, 'Alright, let's go looking for a job now.'

The grandchild asks, 'Where are we going?'

And the grandfather said, 'We are going far away. Don't worry about the long trip.'

The grandchild answers, 'Alright, grandfather, I won't worry. No matter where you go, I won't worry – I will just follow you. Let's just get going.' So the two of them went looking for a job.

They travelled along together quite a way, and they were both tired. The grandfather decided it was time to stop and camp for the night. The grandfather tells the grandson, 'Get off your horse, we are going to rest here for the evening.' And he says, 'Kneel down, we are going to pray.' So the grandson gets down, they both kneel, and the grandfather tells him, 'Close your eyes now – we'll pray.'

The grandson says, 'Alright.'

So they pray, and when they finish praying, the grandfather says to his grandson, 'Alright, now you can open your eyes.'

When the boy opens his eyes he sees a house and asks, 'What's this all about?'

The grandfather said, 'Let's go into the house.'

So they went into the house and saw all kinds of food. The house was warm. They ate, and after their meal the grandfather said, 'Alright, now lie down on that bed and go to sleep.' They both went to bed and slept.

In the morning, the grandfather says to his grandson, 'Kneel down, we are going to pray.' They prayed and, after that, the grandfather said, 'Alright, now we will be on our way.' They continued their journey.

They travelled until noon, when the boy said to his grandfather, 'Grandpa, I am hungry.'

To which the grandfather answers, 'Kneel down here and we'll pray.' The boy knelt down – they prayed. The grandfather said, 'Open your eyes.' The boy opened his eyes and saw all kinds of food, so they both ate. Then the grandfather said, 'Kneel down, we are going to pray.' After praying the grandfather said, 'Now open your eyes.' The boy opened his eyes and the food had disappeared. And the grandfather said, 'Now we'll be on our way.'

They came across some White people, and the grandfather said to his grandson, 'We will ask these White people for jobs – see if they will give us jobs.' So they went to these White people and asked for jobs.

One of the White men said, 'Yes, I will give you work. I would like you to cut down all these bushes that are around us, and I will pay you.'

The grandfather said, 'Yes, we will cut the bushes down for you.' He told his grandson about the offer of work and also said to him, 'This is a big job, as there are many, many bushes.'

The grandson said, 'Alright, we will take the job.'

Before they started work, the grandfather said to his grandson, 'You kneel down, we are going to pray.' So the grandson knelt down. The grandfather also knelt down and they prayed for a long while. They stopped praying and the grandfather said to his grandson, 'Now look at the country.' The grandson opened his eyes and there were no bushes to be seen. The grandfather said to his grandson, 'You go tell the White man we have finished the chopping down of the bushes and that he can pay us for the work.' He told his grandson, 'Don't you take paper money, just accept silver and gold money – then we will go on our way.'

The grandson said, 'Alright,' and went to the White man to collect the pay for the work.

The grandson said to the White man, 'We have finished chopping down the bushes.' The White man looked at his field and saw it was cleared. He was pleased with the work and handed over money to the grandson. The grandson said to the White man, 'We do not want paper money, we will only accept silver or gold coins.' So the White man paid him in silver and gold coins, and he took the money to his grandfather.

The grandfather said to the grandson, 'Alright, you must hang on to one and I'll hang on to the other.' And he said, 'Now we'll pray and we'll go.' So they prayed, and the grandfather said, 'Now as you are going along on your journey, you spread the silver and gold all over the land and say, "Some day the people will pick up this money and they will make lots of money out of it."'

That is why people of all nations, including the White people, are looking for gold and silver today. This is the gold and silver we threw away. The White people and everybody else fight with each other and have wars over the silver and gold we threw away.

Petáni Lake, looking west. See 'Coyote and the Two Sisters,' 'Trips to Petáni,' 'The Road to Petáni Valley,' and 'Grizzly and the Black Bear Cubs.' Photograph by Dorothy Kennedy. ◀

Trees turned back at Nek̲'na7k̲'í7x, on the way to Petáni, where Ntl'ík'semtm's wife looked back and saw her husband. See 'Ntl'ík'semtm.' Photograph by Dorothy Kennedy. ▼

Sts'uwén [dried salmon]. Salmon wind-drying on racks. Note the man standing on the right holding a dip net. See 'Raven,' 'First Encounter with Missionaries,' 'Native Foods,' and 'The Trip to the Moon.' Photograph by G.M. Dawson, 1889. Courtesy of the Canadian Museum of Civilization, Negative #1067. ▲

Anthony Joe's *family* ranch at Sxáxeňx (Shackan), known as the 14 mile ranch and situated alongside the Nicola River. See 'Archdeacon Small' and 'Tellers and Translators.' Photograph by Doug Sanderson. ▲

Hand drummers singing and circling the N<u>k</u>wi7tsútn tree at the N<u>k</u>wi7tsútn gathering in the Twaal Valley, August 1993. See 'Sun Dance' and 'N<u>k</u>wi7tsútn.' Photograph by Doug Sanderson. ▶

Three drums and drumsticks. For the symbolism on the far right drum, see 'Dog Travels to the Sun.' Photograph by James Teit, 1915. Courtesy of the Canadian Museum of Civilization, Negative #30686. ▲

The first St George's Indian Residential School building (1901-22). See 'Old Ways' and 'Passing on the Knowledge.' Photograph by Bea Hanna. ▲

Chief Telhníts'a7 [John Tetlinitsa] and his wife, KwEłEmákst, of Spences Bridge, standing in front of a tule mat tipi. See 'Archdeacon Small.' Photograph by James Teit, 1914. Courtesy of the Canadian Museum of Civilization, Negative #26997. ▶

A s7istkn [pithouse] in the Nicola Valley. See 'Ntl'ík'semtm,' 'Screech Owl,' 'The Country Divided,' 'Simon Fraser,' 'The Trip to the Moon,' 'Coyote Visits His Daughter in the North,' and 'The Boy Who Was Abandoned.' Photograph by Newcombe, 1903. Courtesy of the Royal British Columbia Museum, Victoria, British Columbia, PN 1000. ▼

Man making dip net in fish camp near Boston Bar (pre 1900). See 'Simon Fraser.' Courtesy of the Royal British Columbia Museum, Victoria, British Columbia, PN 5991. ▶

A woman digging roots at Petáni using a k̲álex̲ [digging stick]. See 'Coyote and the Two Sisters,' 'Simon Fraser,' 'Native Foods,' and 'Coyote and His Son.' Photograph by James Teit, 1917. Courtesy of the Canadian Museum of Civilization, Negative #39755. ▶

INDIAN BASKET WORK FOR SALE

Rosie Skuki and her mother, Mary Roberts, standing with a cedar basket display in front of their store, 1923. See 'Making Baskets' and 'Memories of Lytton.' Courtesy of the Village of Lytton. ◀

Cedar root trays, baskets, and baby carriers. See 'Making Baskets' and 'Passing on the Knowledge.' Photograph by James Teit, 1917. Courtesy of the Canadian Museum of Civilization, Negative #39763. ▶

Burial ground near Lytton, possibly that of Head Chief Sexpínlhemx. Note the 'copper kettle quite new with a hole through it' (to prevent theft), and the horse skins 'for eternal life' (from F. Dalley's diary). See 'Sexpínlhemx's Wife Foretells the Coming of the White Man,' 'Simon Fraser,' 'The Coming of the White Man,' and 'Passing on the Knowledge.' Photograph by F. Dalley. Courtesy of the Royal British Columbia Museum, Victoria, British Columbia, PN 881. ▲

Grave south of Lytton. Yadoski, the deceased man, is represented 'carved in wood with the base stuck upright in the ground having a piece of folded printed calico bound as a band around his head and his legs encased in or ornamented with another piece of printed calico of a lighter colour. Various deceased members of his family are represented in carved figures near to his own effigy, his family totem or crest which was a bear is also artistically carved about the grave of which the family was very proud. There was also suspended from one of the poles his gun but having the lock removed previously to prevent robbery; and also for his convenience and comfort on his arrival in the happy hunting grounds are also several brass and copper kettles disposed about the front part of the grave but with holes purposely knocked in them so as to render them unfit for any wordly theft' (from F. Dalley's diary). See 'Passing on the Knowledge.' Photograph by F. Dalley, ca. 1867-70. Courtesy of the Royal British Columbia Museum, Victoria, British Columbia, PN 6573. ▲

Sts'uwén [dried salmon]. Sockeye salmon drying on a pole near camp, approximately one mile east of Spences Bridge. See 'Raven,' 'First Encounter with Missionaries,' 'Native Foods,' and 'The Trip to the Moon.' Photograph by James Teit, 1913. Courtesy of the Canadian Museum of Civilization, Negative #25005. ▲

Roi.pêllst [Blazing Stone] dip netting for salmon on the north side of Thompson River, about one mile east of Spences Bridge. See 'Ntl'ík'semtm.' Courtesy of the Canadian Museum of Civilization, Negative #25004. ▶

Spílaxem (Non-Creation Stories)

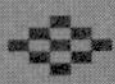

Spílaxem (Non-Creation Stories)

SPÍLAXEM are non-creation stories, which the elders thought it was important to tell. I have put them in loose chronological order, beginning with our first contact with Europeans. These stories include information about our history, way of life, and cultural teachings. I end this collection with a sample of stories that I have heard over the years from my father and grandparents. As the reader will see, many of the stories my grandparents told me are similar to others in this collection.

The Lost Hunter

Told by Mabel Joe
Translated by Dorothy Ursaki

LONG AGO, our people were nearly starving to death. One man went hunting. His friends knew he went hunting, but they didn't know where. He did not come home for several days, so his friends went into the hills and mountains looking for him. He must have been tired and hungry.

The man who went hunting came across a pine tree. He peeled the bark off this tree and got to its sap. He sank his teeth into the tree-sap – he must have been starving by this time. This tree-sap is sweet, like sugar and honey, and our people use it as a sweetener. It turns to pitch once it is uncovered.

The man hunting was so hungry that when he bit into the tree-sap, his teeth sank into the tree. And that is how his friends found him – he was dead, with his teeth clamped onto the tree.

Smuy̓mn (Person with a Cane)

Told by Peter Bob
Translated by Bert Seymour

THESE TWO YOUNG CHILDREN were walking down the Petáni road, and they met up with an elder. This man was blind – he could only feel around with his cane. His cane was his eyes.

These two youngsters said, 'Here comes Cane – let's hide on him.'

The other one said, 'Why? He can't see! Just sit beside the road – he'll never know that we're here!'

The two young boys never said anything – they just sat there and watched the elder come with the cane.

When the old man got to where they were, he stopped and said,

'Heh, somebody around here?' The two young boys never said anything – they just sat still. He says, 'I know you're around here.' But they still wouldn't say anything – they just kept quiet. He said, 'I know you're around. If you don't answer me, I'm going to start calling you names!' But they wouldn't answer him back, you know – they just kept still.

So he swung his cane around until he got to where they were. He pointed at them. He says, 'Well, you won't answer me, I'm going to start calling you names!' He says, 'I know you're sitting by the side of the road!' He says, 'You wouldn't answer me, I'm going to start calling you names – you stinking bums! Worse than that, you stinking bums!'

They smiled at one another, 'This guy's blind – he can't see us!'

'We should show ourselves.'

'How can we show ourselves? He's blind!'

'But we can talk to him!'

'Yeah, we're here!'

'How can you hide away from a blind person?' He says, 'I can't see you, but I know you're there! Now tell me who you are! Tell me your names!' So the first one told him who he was and the second one also told him who he was.

He was going down towards Lytton. He told the young boys, he says, 'Watch me, now I'm leaving.'

He's walking along with his cane. All of a sudden he stopped again and said, 'Oh, you are around here!' And a rattlesnake was rattling. Then he sat down where that rattlesnake was coiled up, and he started communicating with it. He's an Indian doctor. This happened a long time ago along the Petáni Road, before the White man came.

Why There Are Nlha7kápmx in Spokane

Told by Mabel Joe
Translated by Dorothy Ursaki

YEARS AGO there was a couple who had a large family. Their youngest child was a girl, and when she grew up, another couple wanted her to marry their son. The couple with the daughter would not accept the son, so the young man threatened to kill them.

The threatened couple took all their children on their horses and travelled south from Nlha7kápmx territory to Spokane, in the United States. They travelled on horseback for many days, not knowing where they were going. They looked for drinking water and did not find any. The land was prairie, and they could see no place with water.

The couple told all their children to close their eyes and pray. The children prayed and kept their eyes closed for quite a while. Then suddenly they heard water trickling, but the father told them, 'Don't stop praying. Keep your eyes closed and keep praying.' After a while they heard water running close by. They opened their eyes and saw water – immediately, they watered their horses and drank themselves.

After they had had their fill of water, the father told the whole family to close their eyes and pray to the Creator for food. Their prayers were answered – food came and they ate and enjoyed themselves. They stayed at this particular place for quite a while before moving on to Spokane.

I don't know if they came back to Canada or not, but they were not hungry or thirsty any more. They lived happily ever after.

According to stories told by our ancestors, our people have always yámit [prayed] to the Creator, and yet you hear White people say that they taught us to pray.

Sexpínlhemx's *Wife* Foretells the Coming of the White Man

Told by Annie York

IN THE BEGINNING, before the White man came, the Indians had their own religion. At Lytton, Sexpínlhemx, his wife, she went into a trance – she died. Mind you, after three or four days she returned to this life. She was taught what prayers to use and she foretold what was coming ahead, even to the airplanes, cars, electric stoves – even what they were going to look like.

She told the young generation, 'There's people coming across the sea. These people are going to have fire that's going to be inside of a thing, and when you do your cooking, it's just going to be automatically done.' And says, 'There will be things you will never see before – they're going to fly in the air.' And then says, 'It's going to run on the pathway.' But she says, 'I can't describe it to you – what it's going to look like.' But she says, 'The one that's coming is going to be joined together in a long thing.' That was the train. And she said, 'It's going to make a funny noise and you're going to hear it.' And that was what she foretold to the young generation. And it did come.

Simon Fraser

Told by Annie York

WHEN SIMON FRASER came down, of course the Lytton Indians were the first ones that viewed him. They seen this man – the Lytton Indians seen this man coming down in a canoe with his party.

Chief Sexpínlhemx, he soon spotted it, and he says, 'That's what my wife foretold, that that man is coming to this area.' So he said to the Indians, 'You Indians must never touch him, you mustn't hurt him. See that white handkerchief what he has on his head?' He had a white handkerchief tied around as a band, and he's the headman in the canoe.

And when Sexpínlhemx's servants spotted Simon Fraser, he camped down there somewhere around the other side of Cisco [Siska], somewhere around there somewhere – and that's where he forgot his axe, his little hatchet. Simon Fraser forgot his little hatchet. But Sexpínlhemx said to his servants, 'You boys must make it. You must run after that canoe and you must catch up to him and give him his axe.' So they did – they caught up to him and gave him his axe.

Sexpínlhemx told his men, 'You must keep on going to Spuzzum and send the word down there that you must never hurt that man. That's the man of the Sun – he's the son of the Sun.' So these Indians came along and came to Spuzzum and they spread the news all around.

But my grandmother, my own grandmother, she was ten years old, and they lived down there, on the other side of Spuzzum Creek, right at the mouth, and there were several others. Paul Yúg̲la7 [Yoala] was there too, and several other Indians were there. And this special man came in a canoe, and when they seen him they knew who he was. That was the man that was foretold to come along.

And they welcomed him, and they had a little dog. The Indians had fish broiled by their summer campfire in the spring. It was in springtime, and they had this camp fire. They were broiling their fish and they offered Simon Fraser the fish. He didn't like the fish. He kept pointing at the dog, this little dog. The Indians couldn't understand why he kept pointing at this little dog. He wanted the dog. Anyways, they gave him the dog – and what do you think he did with the dog? He killed the dog and ate it. That's what he had for supper, but the Indians didn't like that very much.

The next morning they cooked the fish for him. Then he took part of the fish and the chief came. Then they had their pipe – the pipe was always used. The chief flew his flag and ordered all his tribe, 'You must never beat this new man.' Because that was their traditional way of living. So Pálak, he ordered all his people, 'You must never hurt this man. You must welcome him.'

And so they did and he stayed for a few days, down there by the cottonwood tree. There's a big cottonwood down there by Spuzzum Creek at the mouth, and that's where the camp was. And our great-grandmother was there, and our grandmother was ten years old, and she told us this story.

There was a special woman, she was related to our grandmother. This special woman, she was an entertainer – she was a singer and she was asked to sing this special song when Simon Fraser was leaving. So they had a sort of a prayer, a special prayer for him, that he must be saved in his voyage drifting down the Fraser River. They warned him about Battleship Island. They told him that one of the rapids was very fierce. They told him in a way that he could understand. They pointed, and they did this to the water [she gestures, indicating the roughness of the water]. They made it rough and told him, 'That's where he's going to go through.' These people that was with Simon Fraser, they understood that it was rough.

So when he was leaving they had this party, and this lady singing a special song – a traditional song for him. So anyway, she sang this song, and Simon Fraser, when he was leaving, he seemed so sad over it. He had tears in his eyes when he was drifting away in his canoe, and this lady who sings the song, she says:

> We'll meet you again when the leaves are turning red and yellow. When our chief asks us to pray, we'll pray for you when the sun rises – and when the sun rises, we'll bow our heads towards it and we'll pray for you; and when our Chief takes his pipe and smokes his pipe, the smoke will drift down the river to follow you, and our prayers will descend with you and will accompany you; and when all the trees sway along the beach, the green leaves and the green boughs and all the emerald greens will sway around

> you and the silvery circle – the eddy, the pool – and you'll be safe when you go through this channel. And when we're in the woods, in the forest, we'll always pray for you, and our prayers will always remain with you, and all our tribes from Spuzzum will always pray for you to return, and one day your flag will fly over us.

That's Chief Pálak's farewell to Simon Fraser; and this lady, she's singing that song on behalf of Chief Pálak.

Simon Fraser, when he first came here, of course this was the last of the Thompson Indians right here. And when he went over there – the Indians have a traditional way of guiding a person – so when he was leaving, they gave him blessings, and when he went through Yale and all the way down nobody done no harm to him. He was safe all the way through. I don't know how the chief found out that he was safe. He went and he told all of his people, and they prayed for him again and they sent their prayers to him.

The Indians took him as the son of the Sun. Well, you see, the Indians always thought the White people came from the Sun, and they reverenced the White people that way. I don't know why, but that's the way they used to look at it – in the beginning, anyway.

Indians, when they pray in the springtime, when they get a fish they have a special prayer. When they're going to eat, they're going to have a special prayer, and they must never eat a meal by themselves – doesn't matter how small the fish is, you cut it all into little strips. The old ones are the first ones to eat their share – the children they get the last. But they have a special prayer. They bless their food and they ask God to bless their food for them and give them more and provide them with all their needs in the way of berries, game – and their work must be done without any fear. Their work must be helped by God, so that they may learn how to do things and how to preserve things and how to go up in the mountains without getting tired; and they must make their journey safe and animals must never attack them – and that's the way they said their prayers.

Of course there is a special way of living for Indian children. The little boys are taken by their grandfather and taught by their grandfather. The little girls are taught by their grandmother. She always has a special little place where she teaches the girls. They have a kwickwillie home [a s7istkn or pithouse]. Kwickwillie houses are dug out so far, and the sticks come out like this, and then they have a ladder right in the centre. Well, the young girls, when they become about nine, they take them away – they mustn't live among the grown-ups. There's a special lady that teaches them how to weave baskets, how to weave the Indian blankets, how to dry the berries, how to dig the sweet potatoes that they gather up in the mountains. She teaches them how to cook, how to cook wiỷe [Spanish moss] – that black stuff that they gather from the trees – and they soak it so many days and wash it clean and then they dig the earth. They build a fire first, and when the earth is hot they dig it out and put Spanish moss on after it's washed. And they put it there, put rocks on the bottom, lay sticks side by side, pour the water in, and then they cover it up good. It has to be there for about twenty-four hours.

First Encounter with Missionaries

Told by Annie York

MY MOTHER, my great-grandmother, they were visiting way up at Pennask Lake. They had relatives back over there and they went there. And it was early spring. They went there and they fished. There weren't many fish – the fish were scarce. But they really belonged to Thompson Siding [Nk̲'awmn] – that's my mother's people – same as my great, great mother-in-law. And when they came along as far as Merritt, this side of Merritt, right by that spring – it's a place called Springs, on the other side of Sulús [Shulus] reserve – they saw something coming. They saw this dust coming behind them. And they thought it was a whirlwind by the way it looked, but when they looked they saw an animal was coming and a woman with funny-looking clothes; and when they looked at this, they seen several others with them that was on horseback. And so the poor things, they went and hid under trees, the little children. Their children hid under the trees, and they run away from these people – they don't like to see them.

So finally, they got around them, and coaxed them, and so they went, and the first thing they gave them was bread and butter. And what do you think? They think the bread and butter was fungus from the trees – yellow fungus. And she told us, 'You children must never eat that stuff – that's poison.' She says, 'You'd be dead tomorrow if you touch it.' So the children wouldn't touch it. But no, the lady was so kind to them, that they fell for it.

So all that they could see was an old prayer-book that this woman carried, and she kept on showing it because it had a cross on it. So that's how they could tell that these people must be religious. But the horse is what scared them – they didn't like to go near the horse.

So when night came, these nice people came and covered them with a blanket – and what they never saw in their lives was a blanket! Anyway, they asked them, they made motions to them like this, and they couldn't understand at first what was meant. And the old lady says, 'I know what that means.' She says, 'That means drink.' So they moved them on right where that spring – right below where Shuter's house is now – and there's a little spring there. That place was called Spring All The Time from then on. She took these people there, so they got water and they made their tea. And the thing they made, what tasted wonderful, was the stuff that was made out of flour, and it's cooked in a great big iron pot – cast-iron pot. They just make a fire beside the pot and they boil it. And they couldn't think what that was, and this woman she made something out of this flour and put it into this pot and put some dripping in there, and they made sort of a soup. And she put sugar in there, and when the kids tasted the sugar – that was something wonderful from heaven!

So they led these people all the way down as far as Thompson Siding – took them to Thompson Siding – and the first thing these people did, they took out the goldpan, and the old lady, my great-grandmother, and my great-grandfather from my mother's side, they look at this pan and they wonder, 'What on earth? Are they going to play by the beach?' So they stood and they watched them. They went there and moved all the rocks, and they find these great big nuggets – gold nuggets at Thompson Siding, and they were just yellow in the pan and the kids run home and tell their parents, 'You know these Whites, they are playing with rocks, down at the beach there and they are having a nice time. They're gathering these nice yellow rocks, like this.' So the old lady went down to see and wondered, 'What on earth are they doing with those rocks?' Because she says, 'Ourselves, we don't value the rocks. We don't take them – they just play with it and throw it around.'

So these people – this woman, and the man, and a young fellow – this woman's name was Annie, and the man's name was Louie. But anyway, my great-grandmother, her daughter was called Annie. In fact she was so fond of the name that she called her two daughters Annie. Both of them were called Annie, and the son was called Louie. So after that, they showed them how to wash gold and they told them, 'That's the stuff that you're going to use to buy your clothes with,' and they wondered what clothes that's going to be used for.

So anyway, they cried and cried when they seen these people were leaving them. They left them with food, they left them with clothing, shoes, and a coat – something they never owned in their lives. They used this thing. They never washed it – they don't know how to wash it – and it got so raggy before they seen other coats begin to come in from all directions. They seen different people coming in, different style of people coming, and there was a string around the beach at Thompson Siding and they were mining – washing gold. And that was my ancestor from my mother's side.

The Coming of the White Man

Told by Mary Williams
Translated by Mamie Henry

THIS IS A TRUE STORY of what happened to our ancestors. When the White man first came from Yale to Lytton, they saw lots and lots of people and wanted to take over the country. They brought the rest of their friends, many boats of them, and rowed upstream to Lytton along the river's edge.

They arrived with one of their headmen, and told the Lytton people to gather at the place where the Canadian National Railways station is now situated. That was where they were all to be shot.

At the time, Chief Sexpínlhemx [Spintlum] was in Lillooet, but he sensed that his people were going to be killed. He said, 'I'm leaving; my people are being killed.' He left on his horse, a nice-looking horse. He galloped all the way down to where the Thompson and the Fraser rivers meet. His friends crossed him over and he came to where all the people were gathered. Every one of the White men had loaded rifles, ready to shoot the people of Lytton.

Chief Sexpínlhemx spoke up, asking, 'What are you going to do?' The Whites said that all the old people were going to be killed off – only the young women were to be kept.

'Stop right there!' commanded Chief Sexpínlhemx. 'End that talk right there! I am going to give you some land!' Chief Sexpínlhemx stood up and stretched out his arms to the sundown and to the sunrise, saying, 'This side will be yours and this side will be my people's. You are not to kill anyone. I give you that which is truly mine – and all my friends, that which is theirs.' This is what Chief Sexpínlhemx said.

The White people agreed. They put down all their guns and shook hands with the Indian people and went back to where they came from, back to Yale. Some moved into Lytton and built homes. At one time it was all marked off, but they're gradually moving in on us.

Chief Sexpínlhemx said, 'If you move in any further, I am going to build a jail. I am going to have it built myself and I'll get our own police – you will have your own police. You, the White Man, shall not pass over here, and we will not pass over there and do any wrong.'

The headman from the White people said, 'Alright, we'll do that and you do the same.'

I, myself, saw that jail located in the centre of Lytton. It was built of logs – like a longhouse. It's really true, and it's true the White people are crowding in on us. And that's all I know of this story.

Sun Dance

Written by Bill Walkem

When the Europeans came to this land, they thought Indian people were the savages: 'We must tame those savages.' And so came the spoilers of our people, the 'Black Robes.' Christianity was forced upon us, and God and Christ were the superbeings.

The Nlha7kápmx had a form of belief or religion – like the Sioux – they believed in nature, and the sun was held in the highest esteem.

The Nlha7kápmx at Spences Bridge respected nature, and so held ceremonies each year. They worked with nature and so held rituals. From ages in the past, they have picked out a time of the year when nature was very good to them. According to past history, they chose the fall or autumn as their time to worship nature and the sun.

When they left their pithouses, nature guided them, as they were always in search of food. Fishing was very important, as was the processing of berries and legumes. Every household hunted and stored meat.

Twaal Valley was an ideal place for a large number of people to spend the summer and autumn. The valley had good water, plenty of areas in which to prepare food supplies, and forest for the deer, which, like bison for the prairie-dwellers, supplied food and clothing.

The sockeye runs came in the summer. And there was always the coho salmon influx, which comes towards the end of the sockeye run. When the coho appear, it is time for the hunters to leave the fishing grounds, and most of the people leave to accompany the hunters. Those who are left behind look after the fishing.

We have always looked to the sun as the giver of life. When autumn comes, the berries and fruit are ripe, the game animals are fat, and the salmon are plentiful and ready for storage. To give thanks to the giver of life, the Nlha7kápmx worshipped the sun. They chose a place where there was plenty of space for large gatherings. A tree – a symbol of power, life, and beauty – was chosen. The chief chose a sexwná7m [healer], one who heals the sick, to lead the crowd in the ceremonies.

They gathered around the tree and waited for the coming of sunrise. All faced east. When the first rays of the sun could be seen they started singing and dancing. They bowed their heads and prayed. The prayer, 'Oh, Sun! You were here first! With you, everything lives – you are the giver of life. Help us today that we may be successful in anything that we do. Thank you, thank you.' When evening comes, as the last rays of the sun are seen to the west, those who are in camp pray and give thanks for the day.

This ritual is similar to those held at all churches during Thanksgiving. The hunters would come in with deer, and the meat would be cut up and processed for the winter. The latecomers from the fishing places brought some of their fish. This fall gathering of the people was a good get-together. People were happy when they saw each group, and it helped in getting the winter stores filled. This place where they held their yearly gatherings was owned by my dad's grandfather, Bell. We have no record of his birthday etcetera – but he knew of the coming of Simon Fraser.

Nk̲w'i7tsútn (A Place to Dance)

Told by Bill Walkem

THE LAST SUN DANCE amongst the Nlha7kápmx could have been in the year 1880. We can figure that out as close as 1880, as Nancy Minnabariet attended the last festival they had there. She came from P'k̲aỷst – that's up the Thompson River, about eight miles from Spences Bridge. She nmitsa7k̲wúps [rode behind the saddle] of an old lady who was going to the Twaal Valley and Nk̲w'i7tsútn. She was just old enough to remember and strong enough for the ride.

So we figured Nancy's age at about five or six years old – we figured her age out. She was mining with Lamíṅak at Sp'áp'tseṅ [Spatsum] – gold mining. And Tommy Lick came through visiting, blowing his mouth-organ through his nose, as all young people – just to attract young women. Nancy figured she was about eighteen, and same with Lamiṅak, and placed Tommy Lick as thirteen years old. Now, my dad – Charlie – and myself, we visited Leon Moran's grave, and there was an inscription on the grave: 'Born November 1879.' Tommy Lick was born the same night as Leon Moran. So we figured Nancy's age at five years older, which would make her year of birth 1874 or 1875. That's how we come for Nancy's age. My brother Bert Walkem was irrigating in Twaal Valley at old Bells place – Nk̲w'i7tsútn. He saw Nancy visiting at our place – where dad and mother lived. And Bert asked Nancy if she wanted to see Twaal Valley. She said, 'I haven't been up there for years – I would be glad to go.'

When they got there, Nk̲w'i7tsútn, she got off the jeep and looked at that old tree – the dancing tree. She said, 'It's wonderful to see this tree again! It's just as beautiful as when I first saw it, and that was a long, long time ago!'

Yes, the old tree still stands. I would figure about five hundred years old, more or less. It's a master. It stands, the sun shines on it, and makes it feel lonely for the Spirit. It used to see, and as the sun leaves, it brings back day and night – two to three hundred years ago. At times, when you look at the tree, its history makes you wish the laws relating to it were in writing – but, as it is, we must say, 'Good, living, wonderful tree that you are!'

I tell you a story about the big pine tree that used to be up about a mile from where the Nk̲w'i7tsútn tree stands. That first tree was photographed and written about by Jimmy Teit. I believe it is twenty-two feet in circumference – a great big yellow pine. The people moved from there on account of the grazing for animals and, of course, because of the Nk̲w'i7tsútn tree's young age. People switched to the younger tree. When people, that is, those that have gone, wanted to praise nature and the sun, they picked the most beautiful tree in the valley, and through that tree, hope carried on for another couple of hundred years. I guess that tree was born before Columbus.

Archdeacon Small

Told by Bill Walkem

YEARS AGO, before they had any roads back in to Murray Creek, we used to go on horseback and hunt. We hunted for deer. I asked dad about this trail, the old Indian trail – it's wide, well-used, 'There must've been real hunting grounds for the Indians?'

He said, 'Yes, it's been a real hunting ground here. From here to Wísiyem̓xw [High Mountain] there and toward Petáni. And there's a shortcut from Murray Creek to Petáni – you don't have to go to High Mountain.' He says, 'But Mr Small, the Archdeacon, he used that trail. He's the one that used the trail more than anyone else. Of course, he used to go up and down there – even twice a month, I'd say.'

He'd go from Spences Bridge right up to Wísiyem̓xw. From Wísiyem̓xw he'd drop to 14 Mile [fourteen miles north of Lytton on the Fraser River], go upstream a little and cross at the ferry. And the archdeacon would go to the Adams country – 20 Mile [twenty miles north of Lytton on the Fraser River]. There's a small little church there – he would stay overnight.

Next day he'd go to Stein – there's another church at Stein. He would camp there and visit the graveyard – for some reason he liked to camp there. I guess that is the power of nature, that Stein – one can feel nature at its best at Stein. When the winds blow, at some parts of the day, you can feel nature at its best. Even old Jimmy Teit wrote about it. Chief Telhníts'a7 [John Tetlinitsa] from Spences Bridge, when he was in Stein country, he could feel nature. He has a poem about it – about the training of the young people and their coming to manhood.

After leaving Stein they went to Lytton. Small, he'd hold a service there, and then he'd rest – and when he was ready to move again he'd take the CPR train to Spuzzum. There used to be a lot of Nlha7kápmx at Spuzzum, before they moved to Seabird Island. They [Department of Indian Affairs] moved the Nlha7kápmx from Spuzzum to Seabird. He'd stay down there overnight and then come back on the CPR train.

Next, he'd get on Jupiter [his horse] with his luggage, and he'd go on the east side of the river toward Boston Bar. He'd have Cisco, Kanaka, Boothroyd, and Anderson Creek Indians all on that side. So he rode, and there was no railroad then, you see, on the CNR side – just on the CPR side across the river. And he'd camp at Boston Bar at the Indian church or wherever.

Next day he'd go over the hills from Boston Bar toward Merritt. And, oh! Ma Smith – that wrote a book on the Smith Enterprises – when they were living in Voght Valley, old Jupiter and Mr Small would come in and they'd have lunch with her, and Mr Small would continue to Sulús [Shulus], where he'd camp. And he'd take a trip to Quilchena and stay overnight there – and then he went back to Sulús.

And then from Sulús he'd come down the Nicola River to

Sxáxeńx [Shackan]. Well, there's Canford in between. There's an Indian church there at Canford and at Sxáxeńx. He'd camp at Sxáxeńx, and then, when he was ready to leave there next day, he had two routes – he'd either go to Spences Bridge and then up Murray Creek, west of the Fraser, or he'd go from Sxáxeńx over the hills to Nk̲'awmn [Nicomen] on old Jupiter and then from there to Lytton – either of two ways. And the Indians really loved him – they thought a lot of that Archdeacon Small there. When he died in 1909 in Lytton, the Indians sitting outside his funeral service were wondering, crying, and chanting, 'Who is going to be our next preacher?'

Xítl'ix (Nlha7kápmx Court)

Told by Louie Phillips

WELL, THAT'S XÍTL'IX. That's judge – that's Indian court. They make you kneel down – the chief asks you questions.

You don't talk too fast – not talk good now. They make a fire. They make you kneel down, close to the fire. And they make a big fire and you get burnt – scorched. When you don't talk, they keep you there, close to the fire. You start to curl up. They can't force you to talk. And if they burn you, scorch you, hurt you – too damn bad – whether or not you say, 'I did it.' And then you are through, and then they give you a punishment.

Anything wrong, they put you to Indian court. And if you don't tell the chief what he wants you to tell him, they will put you to high court. They kneel down before fire – that's high court.

But you're going to get punished – you done wrong.

Same with the woman. If the woman done something wrong, 'Let's xítl'ix.' And the woman would get the same punishment – that's the law. That's why the Indians were good long time ago, because you can't get away from that fire if you did wrong – bad wrong.

The chief has got councillors and they got watchmen – they are called watchmen. If they need help, the councillors come and help.

Elders – that's their job. If the chief can't do it by himself, well, he'd get the older people to say what they think about it. They all work together.

The watchmen watch everybody. But if you need help – well, the councillor: 'I'll pack him over, I'll drag him over, I'll clobber him to get him over.' The watchman looks after everything. Seen anything going to happen, watches it happen, going to tell the chief.

The chief tells him, 'Go get him.' If he can't get you over there, he get the councillors to come help him.

You can't talk against those guys. If you talk against those guys, they are going to hold your dick. Brings him back to the chief.

Kneel down, and Goddamn, they get a little stick – about that long. Put it between your kneecap and your leg – little short stick. And they kneel on it. Goddamn! Not very long – that hurt you! Your kneecap on top of your leg! So whether or not you are going to say something ...

Old Ways

Written by Nathan Spinks

IN THE 1940S there was no high school for Indian children. We went to a residential school, where you went only two and a half hours a day for academic instruction and two and a half hours a day for manual labour training (farming, carpentry, and boiler room for boys; cooking, serving, and general housecleaning for girls). These are the things we learned in residential school.

In those times, the people that lived on the reserves had their own justice system. The chief was the law, and when the provincial police wanted to enter the reserve, they had to ask permission from the chief; if they wanted to arrest anybody, they had to tell the chief what that person had done wrong. Sometimes the chief would hold court right on the reserve and solve the problem immediately, for there is no remand in Indian court. The chief would sentence a person right there. It would be up to the captain and the watchmen of the tribe to carry out the sentence. This really worked well for our people – they respected these leaders. Most of the time they only had to go to court once in their lifetimes.

Everybody was equal – there was no such thing as a rich or poor Indian because everybody shared. When you helped each other, there was no money exchanged – the only time you used money was when you left the reserve. In those times, you traded with the stores.

Our people used to grow a lot of beans – speckled beans, brown beans, and navy beans. They grew these beans in vast amounts and exported them from the reserve by the ton. They used to export hay to the Lower Mainland by the boxcar load. The hay was of high quality and was meant for dairy farmers, who hardly used any grain on their herds. That was the commercial end of things.

People used to be self-sufficient. We used to grow so much food that we didn't have to go to the store. We stored our food in the ground or in root cellars. People fished and hunted enough food to last them through to spring. We had all the goodies we needed in our own backyard – if we needed something else, we traded for it.

All this changed when they revised the Indian Act in 1952. That's when they started having elected chiefs and councils. One of the changes was that mainstream Canadian law enforcement agents came right onto our reserves to arrest people – they no longer consulted our chiefs and councils. The DIA [Department of Indian Affairs] started handing out rations. The DIA told the Indians that it wasn't feasible to work on their small farms. That was when we began to lose our self-sufficiency.

The RCMP [Royal Canadian Mounted Police] dismantled the

Indian justice system on our reserves. Because court cases are constantly being remanded, it sometimes takes two months to a year for one case to go through the mainstream Canadian justice system. Today, the RCMP have left us. Their mandate seems to be to police the highways so they can collect fines; they don't seem to have time for the instances of breaking and entering which are occurring in our communities and on our reserves.

We, as Indian people, would like Canada to help restore to us our own justice system. As was the case in the 1940s, we want our chiefs to have authority over us. We want back our own justice system.

Powers of the Sexwná7m (Healer/Doctor)

Told by Tom George and Bert Seymour
Translated by Marion Bent

BERT: There was an Indian doctor from Canford, and his name was Sáplow; and there was another Indian doctor that lived not too far away, and she was a woman. And when they got together they were so powerful – they were so strong spiritually when they sang. This one time they called out the water and the water came in a great big ball. While they were singing, it just went from one to the other. They would be singing there, they would be singing so hard, and their powers would be so strong that the earth shook. The earth would be shaking as they sang.

TOM: I was about sixteen when I was in Yakima. I remember this Indian doctor. I was at a gathering and they were playing slahal. This one guy that was playing, he was cheating, and the Indian doctor was watching him and challenged him, saying, 'I'm going to be the person that points.' When he challenged this cheater, the cheater just laughed it off – but the Indian doctor insisted. While he was playing the bones, they just turned to powder in his hands. Everybody around him was just astounded.

BERT: There was an Indian doctor in Spences Bridge, and he had a brother who was a cheater. There was a bone game going on at Spences Bridge, and this Indian doctor knew that his brother was cheating; he did something to him and he was dead the next morning – his own brother!

Some people don't realize how powerful these Indian doctors are. This Indian doctor was challenging another Indian doctor, and all he did was inhale from his pipe three times. The stronger Indian doctor's power went into the one that was smoking, and the pipe just disintegrated.

On the Boston Bar Trail

Told by Peter Bob

I WAS ALWAYS up in the mountains. I spent quite a few days up in the mountains all by myself. I see things. Before anybody going to die – I see that.

About forty years ago, I was pretty young then. I was way up the Boston Bar Trail – that's the old trail. I was camped out up there, miles and miles away, about halfway to Boston Bar. I was camped out there all by myself – nobody around. Then all of a sudden I heard these people coming. Talking away – and the horses shod – you know, the horseshoes – you could hear them on the rocks.

'Oh boy!' I was thinking to myself, 'I'm going to have company!' I grabbed some wood and put it on the fire – made a big fire. Those guys went on by – they never stopped. I hollered out there. Nobody hollered – nothing. In the morning there was a little bit of snow that day – about that much, I guess [he opens his hands approximately half a foot]. In the morning, I was out there where that trail was supposed to be – nothing. Just the oldtimers going by. Oh, I've seen a lot of things! Beautiful things! And yet I've survived.

Listing to Stories

Told by Peter Bob

MY GRANDMOTHER used to tell me stories when I was a small boy. I would sit and listen, and when I quit saying, 'yi7áy [yes]' she would stop. You're supposed to say 'yi7áy' when you're listening. Everybody was supposed to 'yi7áy,' and then they tell some more. My grandmother was great for that. I would sit there and she would tell any kind of stories – better than the stories you get in the funny papers. That was a long, long time ago. When I was little, I used to like to listen to stories with lots of kids sitting all around. She would tell us all kinds of stories. Oh boy! I would sit there 'til morning – just sit and listen!

When they got together, people went down there and they all sat around and told the same kind of stories to each other – them oldtimers, people from down Spuzzum, Yale – old boys. Then after a while they would get the old drum and sticks out and sing. Sing all night – sing, eat, and dance. I don't see that very much any more. Yep, when I was a boy I used to sit alongside those old folks in Spuzzum – that's where I grew up.

On the Trapline

Told by Phil Acar

A LONG TIME AGO, the people from the Spuzzum Creek area – there must've been 250 people at that time – in the spring they were short of food, so they went digging for roots or whatever they could find, and everybody went except one fellow. He stayed behind in camp to watch – he was an old man.

And the people from Harrison Lake came across. The trail is still there – my old trapline – they came all the way across. They were looking for women. They had lots of food where they lived, and when they found the old man there and no women they killed him – they shot him full of arrows.

So when the other people came home from gathering food and things like that, and saw the old man dead, they sent out runners to Lytton to get the other people down. They wanted revenge.

So they did. They waited for a few days and they went up the trail. They surrounded that village and they killed everybody except two girls – they took them prisoner.

It's true. I thought it wasn't, like they tell stories in the evening, but it happened to be true. That trail comes right across my trapline.

What happened, those girls there were around fourteen years old, and the guy who captured them, he was wounded and he died. And the other guy starts fighting over the girls and the chief says, 'I will decide.' So he took the girls and shot them.

One place there, there's a great big rock there, where I found them. He shot the both of them. So that seems to be the end of the story. But I trap up there. When I look around, I pass that place a few times. In here, by golly, I run across a big buck and I follow him a little farther down past the trail. See, you know the brush there, a guy don't go there very often – and here I saw an alcove, almost like a cave, and I saw some dry sticks standing up. I says, 'Heh! A bear didn't do that! I better be careful – maybe somebody put a beartrap there!'

So I was careful, and I took a stick, and I dug underneath there in that little cave. I only went about six inches and a bone came up. I dug around until I got the skull, and I looked and there was an arrow sticking out of the nose, and I pull it and here was a long obsidian arrowhead. That's royal jade arrowhead. Obsidian, that's a class of rock. They traded that type of rock with the guys from Lillooet. There's obsidian up there. It's very hard to get. Anyway, I wrapped it up. Two teeth were missing, and I counted the cavities in the teeth. I said, 'Gee, it's not a full-grown person!' So I put it in my packsack and I went home and cleaned it up.

I showed it to Annie, my wife. I said, 'Let's go back.' I took the screen and we screened it and we got the two teeth. Here a story came true –

The arrowheads that were for war, they had pretty big barbs. If an arrow went underneath, you were in trouble. Everybody thinks arrows were big, but they weren't. Most of the arrows I found were an inch to an inch and a half. One Indian fellow from Lytton told me, 'They put one in you, you can't get it out and you die.' You have to cut a big hole in you to get it out.

There was one place – I had medical training for a whole year and I forget the bloody thing! Anyway, when you get knocked on the head, you will get fluid on the brain and no way can they take it out. So what they do, in the bottom of your skull – there's no brain there – drill a hole there.

There's a creek up by Lytton there that has a name – strange name, very seldom used. They found a skull there with two holes in it. One hole was healed. The skull had a crack – somebody hit him in the head. They were fighting in a war, maybe. And there was another hole on the other side, about an inch apart, and that hadn't healed, and he died from that – he had water on the brain.

They knew that bit of medical science – I don't know how the hell they knew. Well, the Indians had quite a few medicines, more than the Whites at that time. They had medicines and they could cure themselves. They went into the bush – they had to or they would have died. I got some drills here, very small.

They had to get an injured person doped up. They had medicine. They would make him drink it so he was a little bit out. They had medicine to put him down – and they drill the holes. And one time they drill the hole and drain the skull of the fluid. And the next time it bothered him, again they drilled – and I guess he died. The hole wasn't closed when they found the skull –

My friend used to kill a bear with a big, long flint on a stick. He took all his clothes off when he saw a bear, and he walked right up to it with three sticks in his hand. He burned the ends of them – made them sharp – so they were real hard. They were made from yew wood – that's the hardest wood in the country around here.

Usually if the bear's going to grab you, he opens his arms – he's going to crush you – and he also opens his mouth. That guy was only five-foot-four – he was very short. He was very agile – he was very quick, and when the bear opened his mouth he shoved the stick in and he ducked.

Boy, bears are fast! I can show you how fast. They gave me one hit one time way up in here. I thought the bears were a little slow, but baloney! I covered my face up and it gave me a hit! Anyway, he shoved the stick in his mouth – the bear is stuck – then he would stab the bear. But one day he slipped. The bear had a mouth bigger than his stick and bit him in his arm. When the bear got hold of him, he threw him down and killed him.

Now when you go hunting and you see a spá7ats [bear], he'll stand up. He sticks up his arm. I told my grandson, when you see a bear do that, don't shoot him. According to the old Indian legends, the bear wants to be friendly. As long as you are not two feet away when he sticks up his arm!

I took Carl [Phil's son] up to Skagit – he wanted to shoot a bear. And one ran across the logging road – it was an old one. I said, 'Don't shoot the females.'

'How can you tell?'

'If you wait long enough, pretty soon there will be a cub coming out. Or if you look at her face, her face is more feline – more fine made. A male has big jaws on him – bigger neck.' Anyways, that bear turned around and I hear Carl jerk a shell into his gun, 'Come on Carl, what are you waiting for – Christmas?'

'Ah, he's got his arm up!'

'Well, in that case, do the same!' Carl did the same and the bear looked at him.

Our Tellings

Told by Louie Phillips

AND THEY TELL ONE LEGEND all night – and it's sun-up in the morning and never finish one legend. Now nobody knows, maybe a person knows one word, two words, and that's lost – completely lost. I used to hear it, but I hear so many things – after, I forgot what legend they call that. Parts I remember a bit, but I can't rhyme it together like the old people used to.

Right here across the river – legend there. There's a rock about ninety feet high and Indian painting way up on top. But that's a thousand years ago, I guess. River was that high and somebody stand there and carve in the rock. Now it's ninety feet high. It's that far gone, nobody knows now.

Because old people used to gather, like after a funeral, give him [a teller] a big chair. He sit there and tell legends all night, until sun-up. And I thought they just fooled – can't remember things that good. But I hear three of them tell the same legend and they last that long – from after supper 'til after breakfast. Well, I guess they hear it often, you know, during the evenings – so they now remember.

Well, I hear just a little bit in my kid days, but the old peoples died off and nobody tells it – a real Indian legend. You know, I went to school – we learned something different. We going to tell any of our legends, the teachers wouldn't liked that them days. They'd say, 'That's nonsense!' Now a lot of White people want to hear about it and can't, but that's their fault – because they wouldn't let us do it. They spoil everything. They want their way and forget about ours. So we take their word – we don't do what's ours. When I was ten, twelve years old, all them people who tell legends were gone – so I got left out of it. Well, I hear one word here. The school, they want us to do what they teach us and tell us to forget our ways, our tellings. So there – we lost it. There's no way we can get it back now – it's gone. Ask any of the old ones here, 'Well, I've heard about it.' But they can't rhyme it together and tell it the way the old people told it – it's too far gone. If there was tape recorders those days, eighty, ninety years ago, that's the only way we could've saved it – but there was none of that those days.

I like to hear Indian legends and think about my grandparents – what they used to have, what they used to do – but there's nohow we can get it. You might hear one or two words here and there, but you can't rhyme it together to say that's the legend. White people got it written, so that they don't lose it. They can read it hundred years after and it's right. Indians can't write – when they forget, it's gone. All the old people here [St Bartholomew's Hospital, Lytton] want to hear somebody tell them a legend that they know, but if they don't know it themselves, how could we know it? So when they forget – it's gone. You might hear one word here and there. You ask somebody, 'What did you hear?' Well, they don't know. I often think about it – I used to hear it, but I was too small.

There is just three I know that tell legends. One here was Raymond Dick, and at Anderson Creek there was an old man they called K'ásu, and an old man in Spences Bridge called Sxáysemk̲n. There are only three men I know that can tell a legend all night until sun-up. And I just thought they just fooling. How could they remember a rhyme that long? But I hear it two, three times – the same thing over, over. The old people were smart, they never forgot. Well, after they were gone, nobody tell no legends – no more.

Be all right if we had a tape recorder those days – there was no such thing those days. It would be 1920, I guess, before a tape recorder come in. Because that Jimmy Teit of Spences Bridge had an Edison record-player. And they hear it on the Edison record-player, and they taped in tapes after the records were out. You can't pick it up like the way it was told, you know, long time ago – and you can't rhyme it. I like it, I like to hear it, but there is nobody to tell no more. But after a funeral and after a big supper, the old people sit together around a fire and they tell each other legends.

Making Baskets

Told by Rosie Skuki
Translated by Mamie Henry

WHEN WE DIG FOR CEDAR ROOTS we go up high in the mountains. We dig roots until we get a large amount of them. Then we go home and splice them into reeds and straws and bundle them up. We don't use them right away – we store them for three months and then use them. We gather plenty of roots in the fall and work with them all winter into spring. In the springtime, White people buy the baskets from us.

We look for the trimmings in the month when the blossoms are in bloom. The trimmings are from the wild cherry tree and are red. We gather the thin ones and blacken them – they take one month to turn black. We use wild rose bush leaves to blacken them. We put the cherry bark in cold water and boil it until nightfall or until it looks really black – when it cools off. That's the black trim on baskets. The white trim used for baskets doesn't grow in this area, as the soil is too dry. We go to the Coast to get the white straws for the white trim.

To make an awl, the men cut or split the bone of a deer's hind leg and bury it in the ground for one month. Then we dig it up, wash it, and sharpen it to a point. It's strong. It won't break because it was buried in the dirt; that's what toughens it. If we didn't bury it, just left it that way, it would break easily when sharpened. That's how the old people did it, so that's how we do it today.

We finish our baskets in different ways and with different shapes – we start at the bottom. There are some round ones, some oblong ones, some picking baskets. We work on them until spring.

Native Foods

Told by Christine Bobb
Translated by Mamie Henry

I'M GOING TO TELL YOU about the food we used to eat – that we grew up on. I'm telling you of when we were children.

We went up in the mountains with our parents. There they worked – they dug in the ground. They got everything from there that we were going to eat – they filled everything.

The men roamed around and did things too – lots of things. The horses and all of us hauled packs. I carried the young ones.

Then we went down to our home. When we arrived home our parents made lots of food – they prepared and dried it. My mother dried it while I watched, but I helped her get through drying and fixing it. Then she stored it away.

When it was almost wintertime, my mother cooked it in the dirt. First she dug the ground, then she put down the wood and, finally, the rocks. When finished, the wood was burnt and the rocks were red hot. Then she buried it with dirt – not too much – and blanketed it with fir boughs, maple leaves, and dry pine needles. That's how the roots were cooked for putting away.

They made licoriçe, which they washed in water. It was washed in water until it was clean and had turned white. Then it was put in a basket and taken to be cooked. Everything was cooked this way: sk'ám̓ats [roots of the yellow avalanche lily], tiger lily, cinquefoil, tatúwen̓ [corms of the western spring beauty, also known as wild potatoes]. When wiy̓e [black tree lichen] is cooked it's really good – it tastes just like licorice. They mix sugar with it. Cooked wiy̓e is very good food.

That is what we did when we were children – that was our food. There's the salmon, too, which we dried – and the potatoes.

My parents mined in the river. From what they earned doing that they bought other foods. I mined too, as we all worked.

Trips to Petáni

Told by Mary Williams
Translated by Mamie Henry

IN THE MONTH OF AUGUST, the people gathered up in Petáni [Botanie Valley]. People gathered from all over – Spences Bridge, Nicola, and 30 Mile [thirty miles north of Lytton on the Fraser River]. Lots of people went up there to the flat up at the place they call Red Crown or Top. The bishop came up there too, and joined in the sports with the people – foot races, horse races, and everything else – just like they do now at the rodeos.

Then the people dug roots such as sk'áṁats [yellow avalanche lily], tatúweṅ [western spring beauty], water leaf, and tiger lily; and they picked mountain berries and gathered all the other kinds of food found there. They shot deer and roasted them over open fires. There was lots of fun. They dried their meat and fruit and even made jam.

When the bishop arrived, they made a huge table laden with all sorts of food. He said grace, then everyone ate. There was Mr Small, Mr Pugh, and Mr Good – there were three of them. When the games started, they blindfolded the women to see who would win the sack race.

My, we used to have nice times in those days! Everybody was happy and no one was afraid of anything. Now we are scared when we go up there. At times, good White people would come up and watch the people's races. There would be tents everywhere. There were good times in those days, but not nowadays. We used to eat plenty of deer meat, grouse, and rabbit. Then everyone went home their own way.

The Road to Petáni Valley

Told by Mary Williams
Translated by Mamie Henry

WHEN THE FIRST ROAD to Petáni Valley was constructed, there were only the old people there. Many of the old people worked on the road right up to Petáni. They used hand ploughs, shovels, and picks – these were all the tools they had – and horses. It took a long time and they were hungry.

One day they reached Petáni. They were really hungry, and they killed a horse and ate it. Those poor old people had a hard time of it. That's all I know about it.

At the time they were working on the road to Petáni I was sitting up – I wasn't crawling around yet. Now I am seventy-eight years old.

Ways of the Old People

Told by Mandy Brown

BEFORE, there was no TV, drugs, or liquor. The liquor wasn't available at that time. We had to work to survive and we used to live off the land. We knew all our Indian foods. Well, I do – maybe not everybody – because I was taught how to pick them and how to prepare them. I was kept busy all year round, for each season brought different responsibilities. If we didn't do what had to be done through the summer, we would starve. The ones that didn't do that, they starved – because at that time there was no welfare. Long time ago, there was no welfare, so we had to respect everything and look after what we had.

Homes of the old people – they used to keep them clean. We kept ourselves clean – it was not as filthy as it is now. I just can't understand some people nowadays – houses and everything, they are new, yet they don't keep them clean. They are just filthy – and our people nowadays, they don't seem to respect anything like the way we used to.

Long time ago, we had all kinds of beliefs. My grandmother used to teach me everything – respect this, respect that – and the way we have to treat this and that. It was really good, a really good upbringing.

Memories of Lytton

Told by Edna Malloway

FRED AND BEA HANNA, they'd cook for her. They looked after her until she died – that's how they got that place across the river at Nk̲á7ya [Niakia]. Her name was Mrs Tommy Paul.

Beatrice went to school at St George's with me – her dad was Harry Sam and her mom was Hilda. They raised about seven or eight children, and Beatrice went to school at St George's. After they were married they lived across the river at Nk̲á7ya. Beatrice's father lived over there too.

There was an old lady there – Mrs Tommy Paul. She was widowed and she lost her only son. Beatrice and Fred were so kind to this old lady. She lived close to them. Beatrice and Fred would go over and chop wood for her. There was no such thing as electricity in those days or a tap. They would get water for her and chop wood. Beatrice would cook for her. They'd go across the river and get groceries for her and they looked after – oh, I don't know how many years they kept looking after her. Finally, after she passed away, she must have made a will – Fred and Beatrice got the land where she lived. But she was a kind old lady.

Then, people had no electricity whatsoever, no taps in their houses. They would have to go cross the Lytton CNR bridge to go shop for groceries – pack them over or get a horse to come to the bridge, then haul their groceries that way.

But her dad left a big family – about four daughters and three sons, I believe, and they are related to me somehow. Harry Sam's first wife was Hilda – she was a cousin to my father.

There was a ferry run by Johnson. He left a son – Jimmy Johnson. But it was just big enough to accommodate about five or six passengers at that time. It wasn't until later that they could take cars across. But it's a mystery yet in my thoughts; it's so urgently needed – a bridge across there. They have a better ferry now – but still I think the bridge would be the best thing because so many of our people live over there. And at Stein too, I remember going there when I was a little girl – I guess it's developed quite a bit now, but they sure need a bridge because it's hard for those people that haven't got cars to go across. They got to walk. They got to bring their buggy or horses – nowadays maybe a car – but still a bridge is urgently needed.

My grandnephew tells me that they have a walk now on that Lytton CNR bridge. But in my time you're very lucky to get across without getting killed because there was no footwalk, except where the barrel stand is. Then, water was held in those tanks. I had a cousin walking across, and she didn't know that a train was right close – she ran and ducked into where these barrels are and she had to hold on to that barrel for all her life until the train passed by. I never knew that they now had a walk on the train bridge.

Well, I've been away from home for sixty-three years now, and the times have changed. I don't know the younger people – all the older people have passed on. But I can remember so well.

Our old people, they would walk five, six miles to go to church. Every Sunday, our little Anglican church was shut full. There was no cars those days – they would walk. They were faithful to their church; they would have Sunday School for the little ones. If the parish minister wasn't available, there was my grandfather – Charlie Cisco – or Susanna Dunstan. They would lead the service in the Native tongue. It never failed that these two were always available, and they'd carry the service, in Indian, right through.

My grandfather was a leader for that church. He was partially blind, but he kept the church going. He'd sweep the church every weekend and chop wood. My Uncle Iva and him would supply the church with wood. There was no electricity – they had to use coal-oil lamps in the church, and it was my grandfather that would keep those lamps filled and clean. And my grandmother would tell us in summer, 'Go help your grandfather – clean the church and dust it.' And we did – we'd go and help him out. I must say, our people at that time, the older people, were really faithful to the Anglican Church.

I'm sorry that I've lost my language. I was at school so long – I was at school for thirteen years. When I got home, I could understand, but I couldn't speak it. I would speak a few words and then it would end up in English. My grandmother would speak to us in Indian – she was perfect in Indian. My mother would try to keep us informed of our language, but we were at school so long, where we weren't permitted to talk in our language. If we spoke in our language, we were punished. We had to stay in a corner or our fingers were hit with a bush because we spoke our Native tongue. The times have changed now – after I left school, St George's was torn down and our grandchildren are now permitted to go to the public school. At that time, when I left school, this was unheard of. I had to go to North Bend for my exams because there was no other Native kids taking their exams, and it was only Grade 10. That's the grade I reached after staying at school for thirteen years. There was just three hours of school – the rest was work and play.

But now I'm so grateful the Native people can go to public school and go on to high school and college if they have the initiative. We need some more teachers, we need nurses, we need lawyers and doctors. That's what education is all about these days. We find out we can't get ahead in this world without getting an education. And we need so many of our children to go and get a higher grade in the schools. It was unheard of years ago. You had to be a taxpayer before you could get into a school, a public school – but that's all changed now.

There was Arthur Skuki and Rosie Skuki. Rosie Skuki had a store on the reserve there, selling baskets – I think the building is still there. She sold baskets. The tourists would stop there and buy baskets, roots, and basket trimming. She had that until she passed away. They seem to have stopped making baskets.

The old people, they would use stsá<u>k</u>wem [Saskatoon berries]. They dried them. They would pick them and put them on a mat. Now they use canvas – they don't use plastic. Used to use a Chinese sack, which is not sticky. Every day they would spill their berries on there and they'd turn them every day for four or five days until they dried. They'd package them. There's three or four kinds of stsá<u>k</u>wem, and one is just for dessert – they don't dry it, they use it right away. I guess they used to make a bread out of it. They'd smash it up and dry it and it made bread. But the bitter-roots that they get at Ashcroft – the old people used to boil their Saskatoons for dessert, then they would throw that bitter-root in there and thicken it up, make a dessert out of it. That was our dessert. Gosh, I forgot the name of that! It just grows around Ashcroft, and on the mountainside it is just beautiful. It's about March or April when it comes up.

I WOULD URGE the young people today to try and carry on the wonderful work that our old people used to do. Like digging roots and making baskets for preserving our winter foods. The foods that our old people used to preserve for the winter – they're delicacies now. So if the young people would try to preserve that. Another thing that I would wish our young people to do is to try and preserve the methods of Indian medicine. Today, I'm trying every way to live a little longer, and I'm using roots – medicine that's given to me from my nephews and nieces at home. They talk about medicine for cancer, TB [tuberculosis], and it's really wonderful. Tamarack is one that's supposed to be really good. And there's the ordinary soapberries – sx̲wúsem they call it. The branches and the stems of the soapberry bush make excellent tonic. I have some all the time – year round. I give it out to my friends who think they need the medicine. I don't know if it's a cure, but it's a wonderful tonic. And if our young people would continue trying to preserve the foods and the medicines that our grandparents and grandfathers taught us about, it would be wonderful. Cancer was unheard of when I was growing up – we never knew what cancer was. There was TB, but it's just recently we hear so much of cancer.

Passing on the Knowledge

Told by Fred, Bea, and Buddy Hanna

Spring 1992

DARWIN: Did you ever play slahal [bone game; gambling game]?

FRED: Slahal game, I play it anytime, especially when there's a potlatch – somebody dies or somebody fixes a grave. They play that to pass time. Fire right in the middle, people on this side and people on that side – even ten, fifteen. Oh, it's a good game! Especially in the hop time – every night.

BEA: Way back, that's why the Indians are so poor all the time, a certain bunch would have blankets and stuff that they've made and then they challenge another band to come. And they sing on one side and dance, and if the other party thinks it's worth it, they throw a blanket over or whatever they think. In English they call it the 'gathering,' but in Nlha7kápmx they called it the swáwem. It's the challenge to another band.

FRED: I've played a lot of times. Kneel down, hide it [the bone playing pieces] in your coat or something. The one that's got a stripe around – it's made out of bone. It's got a stripe in the middle, oh, about a quarter of an inch thick. You could see it. One side got a stripe, the other side nothing. I think the side that got nothing, they catch you there; but the striped one, they can't do nothing.

BEA: You've lost if you pick the striped one.

FRED: That bone is tied to you. Whoever's playing, there's two sets of bones.

It's a good game. I know a lot of good songs. Lots of the young boys, they cheat all the time. Just when they know who's going to win, they all join in. What side wins – well, they got to divide the money. Oh, big money too! Anywhere from thirty dollars up to 300 dollars – depends who's playing. Sometimes play all night.

BEA: If the other side goes like this [makes a gesture with the thumb and little finger extended], that means the white ones [the unmarked bones] are [hidden] on the outside [when two people stand side by side with their hands in front of them, hiding the unmarked playing pieces in two out of their four hands]. If they are right, you would have to give two sticks – and whoever gets all the sticks wins the game. It goes back and forth – it can go all night. And if they go like this with their finger, well, that means both the white ones are on the inner side; and then if they go like that, well, both the white ones are on your right-hand side. That's how they play slahal.

FRED: Someone always started. I started lots of times, 'Slahal here!' Everybody sign up – money, money, money!

BEA: They taped one slahal the time Peter Williams died and they had a big potlatch in Lytton – Long ago the Indians used to clean their cemeteries every spring [people gathered to clean cemeteries just as they gathered to hold potlatches]. One family would say, 'Clean cemetery,' and everybody goes. You all bring food – something like a potlatch. Oh, when I lived up there, we always cleaned it every spring.

DARWIN: How did you grow up?

FRED: Grew up with the toughest grandfather you ever had – old Nx̲awléts.

BEA: Oh, that awful old man!

FRED: You don't get up before daylight, whip made out of rose bush – he took the thorns – but oh boy that hurt! You got to jump and run! Just grab your shoes, go way up the hill at Inkesaft [Nk'ats'ám̓] to feed. We had a few head of cattle, a few head of horses – race horses. Oh, boy! We had to look after those race horses! Ah, he was mean – but he made a man out of me. Same with Jenny – she died a few years ago. Yeah, we grew up together.

BEA: Yeah, there used to be a school at Inkesaft – little public school for the Indians.

FRED: I started ploughing when I was thirteen. I was thirteen or fourteen and all I could do was hold on to the plough. Ah, I had a good team!

North Bend, I went to school there. I walked to school from North Bend all the ways to Chomox – six miles every day. In two months my shoes wore out. My grandmother made me moccasins – I used them until I got through school. Oh, there was quite a few people going to school there. There was Jones, Billy, Jenny, Mary – four of them and me makes five. It was a little school – it was a log cabin. After holidays were over I had a chance to go to school in North Bend. I stayed there for two years – not quite two years.

George Stout, he's a big man, big, heavy set – he asked, 'Do you want to plough?' 'Sure, I'll try.' We had a damn good team. Just a little pull, and they just put their heads down and they just keep going. Plough, and somebody put potatoes down.

People used to know what to plant in the springtime. They used to come all the way down to Yale, I think, to get seeds. There was no railroads – the only way through the canyon was a wagon road.

Oh, gee! You go way down, then up again.

BEA: Just a trail, they hauled stuff on horses.

FRED: You can still see them old roads. Old rock wall, just enough for one wagon or buggy or horse. At Spuzzum, near Chapman's, the old bridge is still there – I don't know if it's still there. Made out of wood.

BEA: If somebody went across the bridge there, they had to pay. The Indians had a free pass.

DARWIN: Can you talk about our language?

FRED: Well, the Nlha7kápmx, that's us, we've been talking that language since I can remember, I guess. From Ashcroft that way, Shuswaps; from 30 Mile that way on the Lillooet Road, they all speak the Lillooet language. But some of the people made houses like that [referring to a tipi]. They came from the Prairies and they mixed up with the Nlha7kápmx. It's all different language through that way. Our language went as far as Spuzzum. Seabird Island – that's Thompson – yeah, Nlha7kápmx. Yeah, I got a lot of cousins and nephews there. I don't even see them.

13 March 1992

DARWIN: How does one become a sexwná7m [healer/doctor]?

FRED: Indian doctors – well, you got to belong to your family. Like if you, well – like if I was, if my father was an Indian doctor, it goes in a family. From time you are small, you got to go out with me. You watch me – learn how to bathe, how to do things. As you get older, you start to know what to do, because when you get to be twelve, thirteen, fourteen, you gotta go out yourself, up the mountain. Stay up the mountain – you are not alone. There's the lake, there's the creek, there's the fir, pine, cedar – all kinds of bushes. They are all alive. That's the only companions you'll have. And animals, all kinds of birds up there, up the mountain. Maybe take days before they get to know you, then they start talking to you in a dream, like. Tell you what to do, and you got to follow it – after that it starts to be easier. You got to talk to everything – they will help you. That's how the Indian doctors go. You can look at a man if he's sick, and this kind of spirit will help you – show you what to do, how to cure him up. I could be one, but I was too old. Oh, I guess they were just like doctors in town. You got to start early in life.

That must be something, broken arm, leg – specialize in bones or specialize in the body, cuts.

BEA: They had special people. Like supposing I had a big bruise – they have a special rock, like, that cuts into you and all that bad blood comes out. You gotta know what you are doing, so you don't cut into the vein. In them days, the horse would step on you or you would get kicked by something. You would get a big bad bruise.

FRED: I tell you, there's life in the mountains. That's the one, that's the power you are going to get. Then the power starts building up as you get older. Mostly from the creek or lake – yeah, they talk to you. You can shut your eyes and think what you are going to do. Then you can call him, whoever it is. Come night, he'll come and tell you what to do. There's lots of things you gotta know.

What really happens, as the Indian doctor gets older, there's maybe three or four different people – tribes. They get too jealous.

BEA: They challenge one another.

FRED: Got more power, that guy – 'I'm going to fix you!' They just jealous of one another. Your power gets fixed, and some are powerful. It takes a long time – you got to almost worship. Well, I guess that's why you're up in the mountain. You're all by yourself, the only friends you have is what grows up there, like weeds, bushes, trees, water, lake, and the sun. Sun is the main thing – yes, you worship him. He'll show you the way – he'll show you in your dream, because the sun knows everything, everything that's going on. That's the only friend you got, real friend. They talk to you and you keep building up, building up; and maybe two or three powers you get, maybe one – they all depend on one another. Grandma's grandfather – oh, he was powerful! There were women doctors too – very powerful.

Long time ago, the Indian used to have consumption or tuberculosis. They pulled it [the consumption] out – I watched one [sexwná7m] pull on it. It's a little yellow, almost like an orange. They have a little basket, lined with pitch. You have water in it – that's where they put it. Yeah, I seen it. It doesn't want to get out, its got little legs, like.

BEA: We have to sit in a corner and not even move.

FRED: I watched the Indian doctors – they used to work on reserve. Somebody got sick, you went down and watched. They sing all different songs. After they take the sickness out of the body, it's out – whatever is in your body that's making you sick, it's out. You didn't see it, but it gradually goes away, then you get healed.

The Indian doctors, they don't work alone, they ask God for help. I see lots of them, right before they start. Oh, some of them are good – real professional!

DARWIN: Do you know Tommy Lick?

FRED: Tommy Lick's my grandfather.

BEA: Yeah, he's related.

FRED: Tsawtemxínak, she was an Indian doctor.

BEA: That's Mrs Raphael.

FRED: She was powerful. She was kind of blind. She knew – you going up to see her, she already knew before you get there. No matter how you sneak up to Snakeflat.

Kw'úwa7 – he was the chief of all chiefs, all Thompson Indian chiefs.

BEA: He was really the headman. They never changed chiefs every four years, like they do now. Long ago, if you was a chief, and supposing if Grandpa was a chief and he died, like, before lunch, we would have to appoint another chief before the sun went down. They don't do that now, but in them days they had to or else the other tribe would run all over you. They'd say, 'Well, you have no more chief – nobody stands up for you any more. We are taking over,' and that would be it.

DARWIN: Did you hear about any wars?

FRED: Wars? Ah, yes – Nlha7kápmx always win. They fight the Shuswap, they fight the Chilliwack Indians, they fight the Douglas.

BEA: Yes, they challenge one another. Finally, they challenged my grandfather. Within five days he was dead.

FRED: Maybe some were crippled, but they all came back. Every time the Nlha7kápmx went out, they all came back. They're good fighters – sneaky like.

In 1925, people used to come down, pick hops at Chilliwack or Sardis. Oh, fight! Fist-fight! Especially with firewater.

BEA: The Nlha7kápmx came down and done the fishing for these guys down here. Now if you bring any fish down here, they're all calling blue murder – but in the older days they came down and done the fishing, and the women folks, they worked in the canneries and they went back home. The CNR would take them home.

FRED: Yeah, it's right there where the [St George's Indian Residential] school was. That's where they fight [commonly referred to as 'the battlefield']. They cross over from Bella Coola and all that. That's where they fight – yes, that's the battleground.

12 April 1992

FRED: I'm part grizzly; my mother was a twin [one of our people's beliefs is that if you are descended from a twin, you are part grizzly]. If you, long time ago –

BEA: They were treated differently than ordinary children. They didn't, nowadays –

DARWIN: Did you know about the Bear brothers?

FRED: I hear about them. I don't know how it started, but I think – the way the story goes, I think it's when they started making people out of bushes. Three or four young people going around, 'Let's make some.' People started coming – I don't know how far they went.

My grandfather, he's blind. Ah, he's a good storyteller! We used to look after him. My grandmother went to pick hops and we looked after him. I don't know how he made it.

BEA: Long time ago, the people that lived across the river, dad said they crossed over in canoes – he said they walked three by three from the river, from what they call Hobos' Hollow [Lytton] up to the White cemetery. He said, 'Three by three going up there.' That's how many people must have been going to church there. And they crossed over. They had a church built in Boothroyd, they had one built in Kanaka, one in Inkesaft, one in Cisco [Siska], and one in Stein. The one in Stein is a tiny little church. Long ago, the cemetery in Stein had all kinds of carvings on the fence, like ducks and different things. Last time I was there for a funeral – nothing. The same with Winch Spur. Long ago the Indians looked after their cemeteries. The cemetery at Winch Spur – ough!

FRED: Npa7tsítsi7t, that's a little bear –

BEA: The lady and that boy, like the boy –

FRED: K̲wék̲etl't [Always Smiling], yeah, they were playing around, just the three of them. There was no people here. The little guy, he made humans, and he was a little bear. There was three of them. I don't know which way they went, that way or this way – must be this way. I don't know where they started from. Different places – well, made people there. Good place to fish, that's where they made people. People catch the fish. These three showed them how to make nets, how to dry fish – if there were no fish, they showed them how to kill deer.

BEA: When they got to Lytton, they seen that lady and that boy. They left them because the grandmother spoiled the little boy. She never showed her grandchild how to get the wood. He just done as he pleased and that annoyed the other people because they were always helping – helping his grandmother – so they all left. They told her, 'You don't want to teach him anything. We can't look after you all the time.' So everybody left. That's how come there's a rock with the grandmother's and grandson's footprints in it. It's in Lytton.

Things have changed so much, but there used to be a road goes – like there's the CPR tracks, it come up in there, then you go up over to the cemetery, and then there was the real old road. The road used to go around in here and up around to them houses above the CPR tracks, where the station is. It's in that corner there – but see, it's been moved around.

Like, before, the CPR tracks were level with the highway – but there were so many accidents, buggy horses getting killed and, like I say, Chief McCarthy represented his people real good. What he said went, and that was it. So he must have told the CPR, 'You have to pay for these horses that are killed – the damages, like.'

It hasn't been very long since they dug that through for the CPR. So they must have filled up the fill. And there used to be a house down in that gully there – like the tracks – down in there the road still goes this way. See, everything's been shifted around, so it would really be hard. Goodness knows, maybe somebody found it [the rock bearing the grandmother's and grandson's footprints] and took it! Because the workers, when they were putting in the new road above Lytton, there was a lot of people there. Anything could have happened. They were supposed to've hid it because they didn't want the White people to get it. It is around in there. That's what they done. It's hard to pinpoint it – just where that rock is.

The grandma and grandson – well, they were ready to starve. I guess it would be like a spirit came – they had a little bit of this, and all of sudden it was lots, and when he came, he came as a poor hungry person. She fixed him something to eat – he prays to her and told her she would always get something. I heard that before.

All the places there was – why did the Indians get one acre here, two acres over there, three acres over there? I guess they shouldn't complain, I mean they were just given a week to fence up their properties. I guess that's all that they could do. They had, like a log – there would be a short log like this, another one would fit like this, and another one from that side. That's how they made their fence. So they had to do that. Well, if you had a team, you fenced up a big place. That's what I asked Granny, 'Why didn't you get the full flat?' 'Oh,' she says, 'My dear, we were just allowed a week – the surveyors were already here. We were allowed just a week to fence up our place.' And she said that my grandfather that lived below – well, they'd be down John Sam's, my dad and them. They went up and Arthur's brother, Joe, they went up and they made a sluice from way up, and they skid the logs down. That's how they got all them little places fenced off. Then there was this little place way down. They fenced that up.

He [Fred] lived with the Indians – like from one family to another. He was in North Bend.

FRED: The West Coast Indians, we get them for prisoners. Oh, they used to fight us – Nlha7kápmx. From Yale this way, they used to call them Fraser Indians – used to fight them right here. Douglas, that's the Harrison Indians. There's the Lillooet bunch from 30 Mile that way – it's different. Different language, same ways. From Yale this way, our tribe occupies the land as far as

Spuzzum and then as far as Ashcroft, as far as Quilchena. Okanagan Indians – they're good people. They never fight with us – they're scared of us. They're scared, but they like the dried fish. Well, they got deer meat, lots of roots in exchange.

Oh, you got to see in the summertime at Keefers – there's a trail right up the mountain. Picking berries and they dry them. They play slahal up there. Come down and bring some food for the ladies. They're going to stay a few days, drying huckleberries – oh, they're big!

BEA: Yeah, we used to go up Keefer Mountain, pick huckleberries. People are lazy now, they don't want to climb anywhere. Hardly anybody goes up the mountains. That's why the bears and everything is coming down. They're not afraid of anything any more.

The Nlha7kápmx – they rode the canoes, they weren't afraid of the rapids.

Like my grandfather's sister said she was left at camp and everybody went fighting. She said she could hear them outside, and she went and looked, and they were ready to come in. And she just went to the door and she kept saying the Indian names of the big chiefs – but really there was nobody there. But she was saying, 'Get up! Get up! You and you and you and you! The enemy is here and here you're just sleeping!' They just fled because she hollered it out loud enough. She had to stay home because somebody was sick, and she said, 'That was enough of a scare for me!' She had to holler her head off and scare all the enemy away.

DARWIN: Can you tell me how the Hanna family is related to the Hawaiians?

BEA: The reason why he [Fred] says the family came from Hawaii is – Captain Cook came from Hawaii, and he had Indians with him and, well – I guess they stayed. I imagine they must have come to see what's going on. But anyway, the boat used to go as far as Yale. From there, they used pack horses up into the Cariboo, because it was supposed to be in the gold rush days. Yeah, we seen the poor donkeys going up. If you were prosperous and you had five or six horses – well, you were hired to go. I don't know how much they paid them, but I guess they went. There were just trails everywhere. Like you could go over the mountain and you'd land in Merritt, then you go over the other way and you'd land over in Squamish.

They didn't say, 'Where's my horse?' or 'Where's my car?' They knew how to make snowshoes. You go round and round out of the trees, when it's good and dry – you use that when you make the snowshoes. Everything got spoiled because they don't get as much snow. When I lived up in Lytton, there used to be 108 inches of snow – that's not packed snow. Every time it snowed, my brother, he measured how much snow. In springtime he said we had 108 inches of snow. You couldn't see anybody when you went to town until you were right face to face with them, because there was a little trail.

It was nice – I mean, everybody knew everybody else. If we didn't have much to pack, we helped the other one. Now everything is, 'What are you going to give me if I help you?'

Down here they got this attitude that Indians get everything for nothing. You have to watch everything that you do. I mean, we've never got anything for nothing.

Like, he says his relatives come from Hawaii – like, I can imagine that because some of his relatives have pitch-black skin.

DARWIN: Did you hear about Sexpínlhemx?

BEA: Sexpínlhemx – oh, they said he was a gambler. I never heard my father say that but different people said that.

FRED: Yeah, he was the chief of all chiefs – Sexpínlhemx.

BEA: There was Sexpínlhemx, then there was McCarthy and Raphael. These other guys, like – like McCarthy would be early 1900s.

FRED: There was chief councillors. There was watchmen – they watch everybody.

BEA: Everything seemed to revolve around the church. They had church watchmen and they had church wardens. That's why I say there must be records in the mission house. There must be some left – if they let you look at them. There was more, you know – everybody was registered. There was a fire at the Indian office and over at the mission house. That's how most of the stuff, I guess, got lost.

The Indian people never referred to, like gold, or like money – it was never discussed in the Indian homes.

DARWIN: Did you know James Teit?

FRED: Yeah, I knew Jimmy Teit from Spences Bridge.

BEA: Oh, that's the one that wrote that book.

FRED: He was pretty good – he used to come and visit us. My father used to work on the railroad – this fellow used to live a little ways away. I think he had an Indian woman. Yeah, he was a nice guy. He looks after – if you wanted anything done, you went to him. He will write for you. I think that's what he does.

BEA: The first language of all Indians was Chinook.

FRED: Yeah, if you wanted anything done you go to him – Jimmy Teit. He lived in Spences Bridge. All the Indians went up there. He wrote to Victoria or Ottawa.

BEA: I never went anywhere – I never even went to town. The Indians were possessive of their families. You see, there was these Indian doctors, my grandfather being an Indian doctor – any minute, you know, some other great man would come and sweep us down. So we never went to town.

I remember my sister and my cousin, they were trying to sneak over to the July first celebrations. The night before, he told her,

'Nobody goes to the sports.' So we didn't go. And here my sister and Lizzy – I thought they were over in the garden – and here they were sneaking over to the sports. And they were going along and there was my grandfather sitting at the end of the bridge, telling them, 'Where are you two going? I told you not to go! Go home!' And they had to go home.

DARWIN: Have you ever seen the rock paintings?

BEA: Oh, yes – there are quite a few of them, you know, painting rocks. They have them up in Stein. That's the only ones I've seen.

FRED: I guess, long time ago, after the earth was cooling down, you could almost write anything on the rock with your finger or stick. It all depends on what you are made of, whether you are part Indian doctor, like.

BEA: There's a certain thing that they use. They call it ts'ets'éḵw [markings made from red ochre]. There is some over by the tunnel. You use it for writing. It's red – it will never wash off. That's what they use for war paint. Got to be careful climbing around there now, you know.

My grandmother's brother used to dance with the rattlesnake tied around. Ough! Because you had to do whatever the old people said, you know.

FRED: Certain people will do anything, and everybody supposed to know what it meant, you know. You seen it drawn on a rock – that means you know who it was that done it. The people that done it, it's given to them – yeah, not everybody. You could do anything on the rock, but there's a meaning to it.

DARWIN: Have you heard any stories about the sasquatch?

FRED: They call him sts'wenaỷtmx. It's a human alright, but it's got hair on its body.

BEA: I guess he must have done something wrong in his time, and that's what some powerful doctor must have turned him into – a sasquatch. Because he *was* a human being. The beliefs, you know, they had some of them. You think that couldn't be so because we are advanced now.

FRED: There's such thing as an Indian doctor – fixes things. But the other Indian don't like that – get jealous. So they just hold, can't change them into real human – too powerful, some of those. They don't like the next person to do better than them. That's how it works. This went on until fifty or sixty years ago. There was lots of powerful Indian doctors. Especially from the West Coast. They got too jealous – they don't like the Thompsons.

BEA: They never let the tribe marry into another. That's why Lytton is all, 'You're my cousin, you're my second cousin, you're my aunt, you're my this.' It's all this one big relative – everybody's a relative of everybody else. They should all try to get along.

Canoe Tom, he was a doctor to be feared. You didn't scare them – you didn't have anything to do with them. He was a well-respected man – Canoe Tom. Tommy Lick, he was a kind old man – they had him as watchman. He grew up in Spences Bridge, but he married Mrs Quinn from Lytton, so he moved and he lived on the reserve. Like Billy Quinn and them, their homestead, that's where he lived. He used to look after the reserve. All the kids had to be home by ten o'clock – no buts about it. He just walked downtown and everybody would say, 'There, he's coming!' Everybody would run home. They didn't dare to play tricks on him, like they do now.

I mean, long ago, they appointed one chief and that was it until you died. Long ago, the Indians had respect for one another. But now, good gracious! If they can cheat you out of something, they'll do it!

DARWIN: Do you have a message for Nlha7kápmx youth?

FRED: It's a different world now, you know. Young people now learn themselves as they go along, while, like me, I heard about the old law, you know.

BEA: I don't know, I think they should keep it up – I think they should keep their mother tongue up. You never know what's ahead fifty years from now. When you get counted again, if you can say 'hátsu' [let's go], maybe you are Nlha7kápmx – if you can't, maybe you're not. So it's up to them if they want to continue. I think they should. You never know – the change of government and the change of this, the change of that – you never know what's ahead. It's best to try and keep up with the oldtimers. At least try to keep up enough to be able to greet an oldtimer.

19 February 1992

DARWIN: Where did you go berry-picking?

BEA: Nobody picks any more. People have all gone lazy. People used to go –

BUDDY: For miles.

BEA: Yeah, go up the hills and come down with baskets full and bring it to town and they make pie out of it – and the town people just loved huckleberry pie. But now they won't buy anything – the Indians won't pick nothing.

They don't have any fieldworker [Indian agent] in Lytton. It's just – everybody wants to stay in the office and work – there's no fieldworker. I mean, before, they had a fieldworker. He went out and seen what everybody was doing. Like, you know, if they were gardening, you know who needs help and who doesn't need help – and those who are just getting their cheque and going spending it. But if you get your cheque and do something with your – like, you know, the ground that the house is on? Well, you can help them – but most of them, they just don't. There's some, you know, like with people that are trying – nobody seems to look at them, to try to help them. Like when I was up there, good gracious! We tried to keep our place fenced up, and we cleaned the ditch all the time.

BUDDY: We even walked right from Cisco [Siska] all the ways to Nk̲á7ya [Niakia] with a couple of fish.

BEA: You know, there's things that the people could do. But in Lytton they don't want to do nothing about anything – yet they want to go along with the other bunch of people, you know. Like, if they were in the city – where you go out and shop and come in and that's that. But why should they hold on to their lands if they don't want to do anything with them?

There's lots of things that need to be looked into, but they just sit in the office. When I phone up, 'Oh, they're not in, it's their day off today.' Gee, how many days off do they have in a week? Then you phone again, 'Oh, they'll be in.' I just lost interest.

Like, there's lot of little things that they could do. Like old St George's, for instance – the boys could irrigate it and cut the hay and sell it to somebody that needs it. Then there's that place where they did have a golf course there – but there's so many bosses and nobody wants to do anything.

DARWIN: Can you tell me anything about your father, Harry Sam?

BEA: Harry Sam was the chief of Nk̲á7ya.

BUDDY: There's one thing I'm going to say about him – nobody had any use for him because he never drank.

BEA: He didn't smoke or drink.

BUDDY: He used to walk all the way down to feed his cattle during the winter months.

BEA: Once a day, I mean – so finally I told him, 'You better start staying at the house – at least you won't have to cross the river.' When we had seven feet of snow, the church from North Vancouver sent money up to Clarence Rebagliate to clear the road. They bulldozed the snow right down to where Grandpa used to have the cattle.

BUDDY: I'll say one thing about him – you made sure you weren't on the road when he went wheeling by! All you'd see was just one big cloud of dust, and he used to drive that pick-up – just a-flying down the road!

BEA: There was a little flat on the opposite side – he fenced that up and he had strawberries and raspberries planted there. He done the same over on their place. That's why I say the people can help themselves, if they just try. I had no time to stand around town when I was there – every day was busy. Even the tiny little squash, they were that big – and I loaded them in the barrel, I brought them home, I peeled them, I cooked them, and I canned them. Anything just to put something away for the winter.

We bought our farm equipment from Grandpa William when Aunt Emma died. He was going to go down to the States – he stayed with us. He sold the mower and the rake and the wagon. We never ever used them, but we bought them anyway.

We paid Arthur for fixing the barn – we used to have a barn right up near the ditch. I know now I would have straightened the barn up and put some pegs on the side, but I never thought about it – it would have saved me.

BUDDY: Gee, I used to pick over fifty pounds of carrots just for a dollar something at the hospital.

The walkway just came in. The CNR at Lytton used to get their water from Nk̲á7ya [Niakia] Creek – deal up there, about that wide. As a matter of fact, you can ask your mother about it – she used to freeze, cover her eyes.

BEA: It was covered with tin, and you could sit up there if a train was coming, and everybody walked on the north side of the bridge. Now they made a walk.

DARWIN: Did you go up to Petáni very often?

BEA: Petáni – that's where they used to have all the sports – up in Petáni Valley. They come from all over.

BUDDY: People used to go pick those wild potatoes up there, just like little turnips – red turnips. I was there with Grandma Lishby one time.

BEA: They look just like little potatoes – like marbles, some of them. I don't think they would be any bigger than one inch round.

BUDDY: She used to tell me, 'You're young. You got good eyes,' so she used to tell me in Indian. Grandma Lishby used to speak with broken English anyway, and she said, 'You go watch the squirrels,' because the squirrels used to take them and hide them – and if you found a bunch, you're maybe talking fifty pounds.

BEA: You dig a big hole, about – I guess it depends on what you are cooking – and you put rocks in there – nice rocks, solid rocks, not the ones that will break. Put them in, and you put lots of wood in and you make a big fire. When the fire is over, then you break branches from all over. Not the firs – not the tree – like, you know, branches from – oh, like from the saskatoon – that kind. You put them in there. Then you put whatever you're going to cook there. Then you put in another layer, cover it up like, and then you put the dirt over it and you have a little hole on the side there. I guess nowadays you could use a pipe, but in them days, they just made a place to put water in and you put water in and it steams. You could put potatoes in there.

BUDDY: You don't use granite, because when it gets so hot it will explode.

BEA: They make cake.

BUDDY: It would be like pemmican, I guess. It would mostly be grease and stsá<u>k</u>wem [Saskatoon berries].

BEA: To make a cake, you make a bonfire – ordinary bonfire. Now you could use foil, and put foil there, and put your cake there, and cover it up, and it would get cooked. It's the same as when you make bannock. Well, they never had foil. When the ground is hard, you can go like this [sweeping the ground clean] – and you just put your bannock along there and that's it. Cover it with some weeds or something, just so it doesn't get too scorched.

BUDDY: It's a shame you weren't around when Grandma Lishby went fishing. I used to go fishing with them – she used to bring everything but the kitchen sink down there! We would cook rice in a lard bucket – they don't make them anymore.

BEA: They used to have lard cans, three-pound or five-pound sizes.

BUDDY: Used to pick your berries in it and all that. She used to cook rice and spuds and fish. When you went down to see her, too – boy oh boy! She would have the whole kitchen cooking! She had old wooden floors, and she used to be right down scrubbing them.

BEA: You could eat off her floors, she was so clean.

DARWIN: How did you make Indian candy?

BEA: You get that off trees in the hills – it's the sap from the tree and it's called ntuw̓. You just peel it with a knife and it comes off. It's good to eat but it's not good to eat too much of it. The trees up on the mountains – pine, fir, then way up, really up in the hills, they had the jack-pine.

BUDDY: Grandpa Thomas used to get his knife out – in the spring you could just peel the bark back and then you get that flesh part and then you just peel it off. Plus you can make gum out of the pitch – that's another thing he taught me. You get a special chunk of pitch and you put it in your mouth and chew on it and make gum out of it. Mine, I tried it later, but there's a certain type you got to get – I got the wrong type. My mouth taste like cod oil.

BEA: Not the fir – it's the pine. The sap would be on the jack-pine.

BUDDY: Something else which you should learn, which I've used a few times. The pitch – you can use it as a poultice. Not the clear but the white type of pitch – and put it on the bandage and stick it on wherever you got a cut or a bruise or something, and it draws all the poison out.

BEA: You have to be real careful you don't put that on your finger if it's hot, because it seems to get hotter. I guess from your body it gets hotter. You just work on it first – we usually put it on brown paper, because if you put it on cloth it would just come through.

BUDDY: That's what they call ts'itl' [pitch].

BEA: But that is a good tonic. Pitch – just ordinary pitch. They usually boil it down, and it goes, like, halfways, and then they fill it and boil it down and take it as a tonic. Oh, the old people, they tried everything when they were sick. They were scared to go to doctors.

BUDDY: Well, look at that stuff that, I think it was Grandpa Harry, got for Peter Forbes – he had skin cancer. Apparently there's this special place that you get that special stuff. Peter Forbes lived how long after that?

BEA: Yeah, he got better.

BUDDY: Some kind of Indian medicine – you find it by the creek, up in the mountains. There's so many things a person can learn. The only trouble, like Grandma was saying, all the people have passed away.

BEA: Not only that, even if you did – like supposing I was to tell you, 'You to do this and you do that.' You'd say, 'Crazy, who wants that? The hell with it!' That's the attitude now – nobody wants to take traditional medicine. Everybody just stumbles to the doctor or the hospital.

DARWIN: What foods did you used to eat?

BUDDY: One of the nicest meats I ever had, which is rare, is rattlesnake meat. It's really good – it's just like trout, but you skin it. Even when the snake is dead you can't trust it, so you have to hook its head down – without damaging the cheeks, because that's where all the venom is. And just cut a little notch and peel it back like that, and the skin comes all off. Put the rest in butter or whatever and fry it.

BEA: Kw'úna [aged salmon eggs] – Grandma used to have them. It stinks – it's just like cheese. You bury it in the dirt, but you don't just get it and bury it. You kind of lay it on a log or something, because when you first get it out of the fish, it's all soft. Then you put it in with them big green leaves that you see by the river – lay them on that and put them down and cover it and lay more on it up to the top. You leave it so long. That's the most wonderful thing for an oldtimer, but keep it away from me! I don't like the stink! It's like that cheese that they get from the old country – it smells like fish. It really smells, but they say that it's really nice to eat.

BUDDY: Grandpa Thomas showed me how to cook a grouse the old Indian way. You get it in clay – leave all the feathers on it. You just wrap it up in clay and stick it in a fire. I just looked at it – I was so hungry I didn't care. And we went up berry-picking. Like Grandma will tell you, back in them days, we used to go for miles up the hills just to get sx̲wúsem [soapberries].

BEA: I went up with Rexie and the damn horse went and left me. I got down to the gate and there he was bumming at the gate and I told him, 'You can stay at the gate.' I says, 'You haven't earned your feed.'

BUDDY: Rexie was something else. If you took him up the mountain, wherever you pitched him up at, he'd eat everything that was around – trees and everything. That's why we used to call him the pig. He was a good cow pony though. You didn't even have to steer him – all you had to do was hang on for dear life.

BEA: All you had to do was point at the one you wanted to catch and let Rexie go.

BUDDY: Being as he was so lazy, he wanted to get the job over with – and he'd actually bite the animals on the rump. Gee, that horse must've been old! I think all the kids that there ever was learned how to ride on Rexie!

DARWIN: How do you make cedar-root baskets?

BEA: Gathering roots for cedar-root baskets. There would be a cedar, and you don't dig right at the tree – you have to go away from the tree, because if you get it too close to the tree, it'll break. You have to go quite a ways out and then you dig – you can almost see them.

BUDDY: Granny used to use a k̲álex̲ [digging stick] – it's sort of like a cane with a handle up on top of it. You just stick that in the ground and you just lift it up.

BEA: The ones so thick, the ones that are really thick, you use them for the inside of the basket. You'll soon find out when you take the skin off and you break it in half – you'll know which ones you're going to use. Splice them up for the inside. And, like the ones, little thicker than that, I guess – they would be the stretchy ones – they would be the ones from way out like. But the ones closer to the tree – they just break.

BUDDY: Then you have to cut it and soak it. Granny used to leave hers in the well – we had a little ditch.

BEA: Yeah, it's best as soon as you get it home to try and take the skin off, because if you don't, they get red. Then you curl it up and hang it up. And when you're ready to use it, then you can soak it.

BUDDY: Same with your basket design. That was one of my jobs when I was a little kid – to go up with Granny to the wild cherry trees and get the bark off.

BEA: Any kind of cedar tree – the bigger the tree, I guess, the more roots it would have. I never seen them dig around the real thin ones. For a real thin cedar tree – like if there's lots of kids with you – you tie that on the end and you tell them to jump up and down on it – pull it and swing, pull it and swing. Do it all day long, and then you cut the bottom off and it will all splice. It will all go like this – then you take it, all undone, and you can use it for the bottom of your basket. So you don't have to use too much cedar – you just cover that up. The cedar tree, the one that's standing, if it's small, you know, you could get the kids to jump on it – tie it up, you swing it back and forth. That was our job, so I know. End of the day, you just cut it down – you peel it and it will just splice up and then you just splice it and hang it out to dry. Then when you need it, you can use it for starting a basket or for putting the lid on. There's a lot of ways you can use cedar.

Usually we used to go up Petáni. It's good going too, up in Salmon River. That's where Susanna [Swartz] wanted us to take her, but – well, as you know, our truck had been sitting for how many years? We never got to go. It was too bad – we could have got lots of things, learned lots of things.

Like when I was growing up, I never went anywhere, never did anything. Like I say, my middle name was 'work.' I used to get up – we'd be all at the breakfast table – and my father would say, 'Do this, do this, do this.' And as soon as he stood up, we stood up too and just collected the things up, covered everything, and we were off over to the ranch. I even sat on the mower and cut the hay – raked it. My brothers and I would haul it in.

One time, my sister, she hit the horses with an apple because she was mad because we wouldn't put her on it. She hit it with an apple – it ran. The horse ran all over the field. You wouldn't believe it! Must've been like from there to over to that end of the barn door where we lost the load, and we had to fork it and carry it in from there! That was a job just wasted!

BUDDY: You should have seen Uncle Handy. He used to just have the one arm, and he used to do all that work! He was a crack shot, too.

BEA: You planted lots of potatoes. You were always hopeful that somebody would want to buy potatoes from the farm. So you planted maybe a sack, and then you hoed around where the potato was and then you got the horse to cultivate it – up and down.

Go in May for cedar roots – that's a good time, when the sap is running. You could go just like this and all the skin would come off and it's really white, it's really nice.

BUDDY: Well, Granny and I used to just go down to Nk̲á7ya [Niakia] in the flats down there.

BEA: I mean, you just don't go, 'Oh, there's a cedar tree there! I'm going to go get its roots' – and there's a pile of rocks and everything! What type of roots are you going to get from that? I mean, you have to use common sense. You just don't go and start digging – you look and see. Some places have nice black soil and you can just start, and you just go like this, and they just come out of the ground themselves.

You'll see a black mark [on the cedar root] and you cut it and you go like this [holding one end of the root between the teeth and pulling it into strips]. You got to guide it yourself as you break it apart. You go like this. When it's going too much one way – well, you pull it over the other side. It just goes down – you got to just watch what you are doing until you get to the end. Then you have to cut the other one in half. Then you do that. Then the one that's right in the centre, you take that off. Then other ones, they'll stay flat, and you use them for the outside of the basket. But the ones in the middle, you use them for inside the coils. Use your teeth when you're doing the ones for the outside, because you bite on them and you have to use your judgment. If it's going too thin on one side, well, you push it over on the other side – that's how you get. That's the one for the outside of the basket.

BUDDY: There's a real art to that.

BEA: Some of them are real good at it.

BUDDY: They use part of the deer leg to make a sx̱we7úlh [awl]. It's all sharp.

BEA: You saw that in half – that's what they use for the awl.

BUDDY: They will push the hole through [a coil of cedar roots] and thread it [through the centre of the coil with cedar-root thread]. As soon as you get it on, when you think that it's tight, you tap it.

BEA: It's always better to have a nice heavy awl because you don't have to pull too hard – because you can hit it with the awl.

BUDDY: Oh, I used to watch Granny do all that! She'd be trying to explain to me – she would have the other piece of the cover in her mouth and I couldn't understand what she was saying.

BEA: She had two little teeth, and that's all she had to bite her roots with. If you do well, you get a real solid basket like the one Buddy's got. It will never go out of shape – it will hold its shape.

BUDDY: We had baskets up the ranch that we used for everything – packing dirt, packing spuds, picking berries.

BEA: Even for putting on a horse. Yeah, that's how that one that Mary has – that's how it got all full of holes, because Granny used to put it on the horse. And when you are going along and the horse is not careful it walks into a twig, and it makes a hole in the basket. Brought my basket back and, 'Oh! What did you do?'

DARWIN: How do you start a basket?

BEA: Starting a basket – I usually tie the end. Some people just put it in two and start working. You wind the thing around. Oh, it takes quite a while – maybe you go one round a day – takes a long time.

DARWIN: How do you make the baskets waterproof?

BUDDY: To make anything waterproof, the first thing you have to do – if you want it waterproof – you just soak it in water and it expands.

BEA: I don't think the baskets leak, because all the baskets that the people make, they used to cook out of them. Yes, they just put the food in and the water, and they put a rock in and it starts to boil and they take the rock out. If they don't think it's cooked – well, they put in another rock. I mean, the White people, they think they helped us out an awful lot.

BUDDY: Yeah, like this one White guy was trying to tell me that it was the Whites who taught the Indians how to cook.

BEA: How to make bannock, he says!

BUDDY: I said we were making that years and years ago. I said, 'If it wasn't for us over here ...' I said, 'You guys wouldn't have survived without learning our ways.'

BEA: Like that Indian lady [referring to poster] – that's in Buddy's room there – she was the one that guided the White people, showed them what to eat, what to dig up to eat or they would have died of starvation. But she was patient with them. She packed her baby on her back, and she showed them, and she stayed with them. The reason why they fixed that, because after she got real sick, all those that she helped, they never, ever known she lived and she died. That's why I said there's a story about her in the book. I always meant to go and get it, but I never got as far as the library.

DARWIN: How do you get the different colours in the design?

BEA: Different colours for the baskets – they come from plants by the riverside. Like the lakes – like they get them like corn – they grow like what you call bulrush weeds.

BUDDY: It's the same with your cherry bark – the darker you want it, you just leave it. But soon as you start scraping it – you get your knife out and you scrape the skin – then it gets lighter and lighter.

BEA: To dye baskets you use – I think it's the fir. You boil that and you put that cherry bark in and then you have to dry it on a rock.

And then when you find out it's not enough – you stick it in again. And that's how they got the cherry bark black – or you can have it brown. But the white for patterns, that's from the bulrushes by the river. Well, they went certain places for that – you never see any around Lytton, but I guess when they went up by the lakes they must have found some because they brought them out and then they dried them. They usually got them around Merritt – I know my aunt used to bring them down. You boil the fir boughs and anything that you can get hold of – you stick it in, boil it, then you put that stuff in and you leave it and then you dry it out on a rock. If it's not black enough, you put it back in again. I know it had something to do with the fir boughs – but there must've been other things.

Oh, you have to cut that [the cherry bark] in little strips. Then you put that in [with the cedar root as you weave], then you fold it, put it under next, then you do that, you go like that, and you have two markings. Like if you just want one marking, you put it in like that – put that top part in, pull it through, then you turn it over. It would be just like sewing. To make the next one, you just fold it, like. So when you are fixing the red, you have to – you don't just leave it the way you take it off – you soak it and scrape it from the underside, get it soft, like, so it's easier to put in.

You just figure the pattern out on a piece of paper and you follow it. It's like everything else – if it's a round one, see how big it is, measure it around and divide it up so you know how many you have to put on. You don't just start in and do this for so many rounds.

BUDDY: Well, something that's very important too, that you have to remember, you can always tell where a person comes from by their baskets – you can tell exactly from what area of the country they come from. Because usually it's somebody that's taught them – you know, taught them how to fix the baskets, and that same little type of design would be sort of a trademark so that you can tell if somebody comes from Kamloops, Williams Lake, or Lytton.

DARWIN: How do you tan hides?

BUDDY: I used to help Granny fix her hides. Oh, it used to stink! Because you have to soak it, and then you put it on this log, then you scrape it all down, then you have to put it on this frame. Punch it for hours – punch it with a special thing with a handle on it. Then, to finish it all off, you had to make a fire out of pine cones. K'áṁa – that's pine needles. But boy, it used to stink! Well, I think the part that made it stink so bad was the brain – to make it last for a while.

BEA: You boil that brain with water, then you dip the hide in. As soon as it comes off the deer, the next day like, get a draw knife. You have to go like on a slant, so you don't cut into it. Well, that would be like, I guess like your skin that has to come off. If you don't take it off – forget it! You might as well throw it away!

BUDDY: You have to clean off all the meat on it.

BEA: Then you scrape all the meat off. If it doesn't come – well, you put it in the water. That's why I say try to do it right away – you have to get it all cleaned off before it stinks. You have to get a log with no limbs. You flip the hide over and you just keep on – you just keep moving it until everything's off. If you skin the deer good you won't need to do much with the insides. You don't use a knife when you are skinning a deer – you use your fists. You hang the deer up, the skin just falls off – you just punch it and it all falls off.

BUDDY: You just pull it off.

BEA: You put it in with the brain. If you don't have the brain, you can put soap in. If you are smart, you'll save the brain of the deer and boil it up and soak the hide in that. The next day you string it. You make little holes around the edge, you string it to a frame, then you go at it – you punch it. It will be tight at first. You are supposed to get it loose, and you tighten it up again – go at it and it will get real soft. If it doesn't get soft, forget it! It's no good for anything – throw it away! You have to work on it. You just don't go like this and say it's done. You'll feel it – it'll be soft and it will stretch out. You got to stretch it right out. When your moccasins or gloves get wet they'll get hard – just like the way it was before you put it in on the frame. The best part is to work on it.

After you get it all straightened out, then you dig a hole and you put in an old log that has turned yellow. You put that in there and you make a fire. Get some bushes that are easy to bend and put them over the hole that you've made. And you keep moving the hide around. Not on the inside part – on the outside part. The more stinky it gets the better it is. I mean it will blow off afterwards, but the general idea is to keep it so it doesn't shrink back to its original size. You have your frame done and you just stick it over and you light the fire. It smokes – you can't see nothing at all. You just keep moving the hide around until you think it's all been scorched. There's no fire, there's just smoke. That stuff there doesn't burn, it just smokes. It'll be white over here – you move it over that way.

Tellers and Translators

The photographs here show some of those who told the tales and who translated them. It was unfortunately not possible to show all the tellers. The biographical sketches that follow provide a short description of the tellers and help to put their stories into context. They are based on Mamie Henry's and Darwin Hanna's personal relationships with both the elders and their families.

Photograph by Darwin Hanna

Phil Acar

Photograph by Jennifer Jmayoff

Hilda Austin

Photograph by Jennifer Jmayoff

Marion Bent, translator, splitting cedar root.

Photograph by Doug Sanderson

Tom George

Photograph by Doug Sanderson

Herbert (Buddy) Hanna

Photograph by Doug Sanderson

Bea Hanna

Photograph by Doug Sanderson

Fred Hanna

Photograph by Doug Sanderson

Mamie Henry

Photograph by Doug Sanderson

Herb Manuel

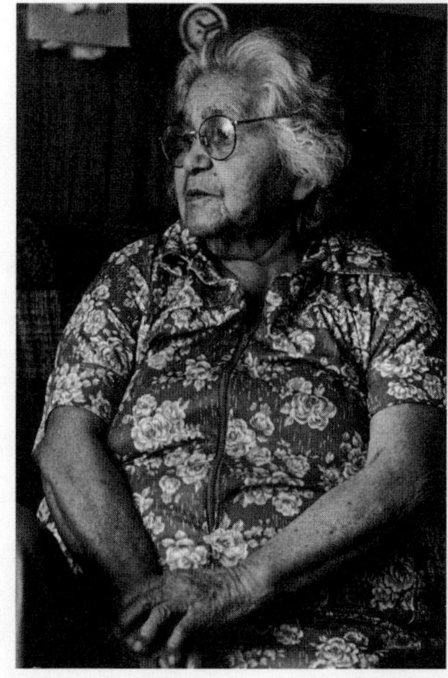

Photograph by Doug Sanderson

Edna Malloway

Photograph by Doug Sanderson

Mildred Michell

Photograph by Jennifer Jmayoff

Louie Phillips

Photograph by Doug Sanderson

Bert Seymour

Photograph by Doug Sanderson

Nathan Spinks

Photograph by Doug Sanderson

Dorothy Ursaki, translator

Photograph by Doug Sanderson

Bill Walkem

Photograph by Jan-Marie Martell

Annie York

Phil Acar

Phil was born in 1914 in East Flanders, Belgium, and was raised in Saskatchewan. After being discharged from the Canadian army, he met his wife-to-be, Annie, in Revelstoke. Annie is from the Spuzzum Indian Band. They moved to Yale, where, in 1946, Phil began trapping up Spuzzum Creek. Phil has learned much about Nlha7kápmx ways from trapping with Annie's brothers and from interacting with Nlha7kápmx along the Fraser Canyon. He has even learned to speak some of our language. Today, Phil still runs a trapline up Spuzzum Creek.

Hilda Austin

Hilda (1912-1993) was born in Sxáxeňx (Shackan) and is a member of the Lytton First Nation. She and her sister, Mildred Michell, lived with their grandmother in O'Keefe, near Vernon. In 1928 Hilda moved to Sísk̲a7 (Siska), south of Tl'k̲émtsin (Lytton), to live with her husband, Charlie Munroe. They moved to Stein in the early 1940s and raised five children. Hilda taught both Native and non-Native people Nlha7kápmx traditional ways, especially how to gather and preserve Nlha7kápmx foods. She was prominent in the Anglican Church, leading congregations in hymns and prayers in Nlha7kapmxtsín. Indeed, she led people in songs and prayers at most of the dinners, gatherings, and celebrations held in Tl'k̲émtsin.

Peter Bob

Peter (b. 1914) was raised in Spuzzum. He attended Kamloops Indian Residential School for ten years. Later, he settled in Nts'alhetkwo (Coldwater) and had six boys and six girls with his wife, Ada. He worked as a cowboy at the Douglas Ranch for eight years, and he logged throughout Nicola Valley until he retired. Peter served one term as a councillor for the Coldwater Indian Band, and he is an active member in its elders' group. He likes to reminisce about the old days along the Fraser Canyon and to tell Coyote stories.

Christine Bobb

Better known as S7ámteka, Christine (1890-1984) was raised in Nk'ats'ám̓ (Inkesaft, north of Boothroyd) but later moved to Boothroyd. She was a member of the Boothroyd Indian Band. Christine was well known for her cedar-root baskets and filled orders from all over the country for her cedar-root cup and saucer set. Her work has been included in Uli Steltzer's *Indian Artists at Work.*

Mandy Brown

Mandy (b. 1924) was raised in Nk'ats'ám̓ (Inkesaft, north of Boothroyd). She later moved to Tl'k̲émtsin (Lytton) and married Charles (Mike) Brown – together, they raised seven boys and four girls. Before she retired, she was a social worker and councillor for the Lytton First Nation. Her special hobby is making cedar-root baskets, for which she harvests her own materials. Another interest Mandy has is gathering and preserving Native foods. She still uses a lot of traditional medicines. When she has some free time, she enjoys travelling to Reno. Today, Mandy is a founding regent of the Mestanta Technological Institute in Tl'k̲émtsin. Some of the clothing she has made is on display at the Canadian Museum of Civilization.

Tom George

Tom (b. 1932) was raised in Nts'alhetkwo (Coldwater) and is a member of the Coldwater Indian Band. As a child, he trained in the sweathouse and in the mountains, and he helped his grandfather with chores on his ranch. In the summer, he fished for salmon; in the fall, he hunted. He has two girls from his first wife, and two boys and one girl from his partner, Doris Antoine, with whom he resides in Nts'alhetkwo. Tom is an avid fisher and hunter. He learned his stories from his grandfather, Charlie Jules, who told stories at all the gatherings. Tom is an active member of the elders' group in Nts'alhetkwo.

Fred, Bea, and Herbert (Buddy) Hanna

Fred (b. 1911) is from Kanaka Bar and Bea (b. 1914) is from Nk̲á7ya (Niakia), near Tl'k̲émtsin (Lytton). They are members of the Lytton First Nation and they are Darwin Hanna's grandparents. Together, they raised six children and lived in Matsqui, Sedal, and Sísk̲a7 (Siska) before settling down in Nk̲á7ya. In October 1994 they celebrated their sixty-second wedding anniversary. Fred worked for the CNR and, later, for the BC Department of Highways. Bea cooked at St George's Indian Residential School and also cared for numerous relatives. In 1974, she and Fred retired to Langley, where they still reside. Despite her arthritis, Bea continues to knit blankets and clothing for her great-grandchildren. Buddy (1942-95), Darwin's father, resided in Langley, where he cared for Fred and Bea. Buddy worked as a carpenter, an iron worker, and a welder.

Walter Isaac

Walter (1904-1980) was born and raised in Boothroyd, near Tk̲wayáwem (Boston Bar). He moved frequently during his lifetime, finally settling in Boothroyd. He and his wife Minnie had seven children. Walter was a carpenter, but most of his life he trapped. He had traplines on both sides of the Fraser River, as far as the Stein Valley. He was also a great hunter.

Anthony Joe

Anthony Joe (1890-1983) was born and raised at Sxáxeňx (Shackan). He worked for the Shackan Indian Band for many years, both as a chief and as a councillor. He worked twenty-seven years for the CNR, and, much of his life, he ranched at 14 Mile (Sxáxeňx), where his family now lives. Anthony also owned cattle and a few race horses. After he retired, he continued to hunt and fish.

Mabel Joe

Mabel was born in Sulús (Shulus) in 1917 and is a member of the Lower Nicola Indian Band. She attended St George's Indian

Residential School, where she met Willie Joe, who was from Spápiyem̓ (across from Tl'k̲émtsin [Lytton] on the west side of the Fraser River). In the 1930s they married and moved to Sulús, where they raised eight children. Mabel has been very active in helping to ensure the continuance of the Nlha7kápmx language and culture, and she teaches in the Merritt-area schools. She has provided invaluable information to many people who were researching Nlha7kápmx language and culture. She still weaves cedar-root baskets, prepares sp'áts'en, tans hides, and gathers foods for winter. She can often be seen at the numerous gatherings throughout our territory.

Edna Malloway

Edna was born in K'k̲émtsin (Spences Bridge) in 1907 and was raised in Tl'k̲émtsin (Lytton). She attended All Hallows School for Girls in Yale and St George's Indian Residential School. Her parents are Matilda (Cisco) and Willy Duncan of Sísk̲a7 (Siska). On a trip with some relatives to pick hops in Chilliwack, she met her future husband, Chief Richard Malloway of Sardis. They raised a family of seven on their dairy farm in Sardis. Today, she sews blankets and comforters for charitable causes. Even though Edna has been away from Tl'k̲émtsin for many years, she still clearly recalls her family history.

Herb Manuel

Herb was born in 1937 and raised at Spax̲mn (Douglas Lake), near Merritt. He speaks both the Nlha7kápmx and Okanagan languages, and is a descendant of an hereditary chief at Douglas Lake. When he was a child, he attended Kamloops Indian Residential School. He has worked as a ranch hand, logger, and band manager; he was a chief for seven years and a councillor for ten years for the Upper Nicola Indian Band; and, for seven years, he taught Native Studies at the N'kwala School in Douglas Lake. He learned many stories from his father and his maternal grandmother; he also learned stories at funerals and at summer fishing camps. Today, he helps with language development and enjoys telling stories.

Mildred Michell

Mildred, known as 'Mím̓li' to her friends, was born in Sxáxen̓x (Shackan) in 1911. With her sister, Hilda Austin, she moved at the age of four to O'Keefe, near Vernon, to live with her grandparents until she was fifteen. On a visit to Sísk̲a7 (Siska) to stay with her aunt, she met her future husband, Albert Michell. They had four daughters and three sons. Mím̓li is a member of the Siska Indian Band, and she still lives in Sísk̲a7. She enjoys playing bingo and attending gatherings.

Louie Phillips

Louie (1905-1993) was known to everyone as S7áa7 (Crow). One time, Mamie Henry asked him, 'How did you get such a name?' Louie chuckled and said, 'Oh, after I was born, the first thing my mother saw when she went outside was a crow.' Louie was raised at 11 Mile, north of Tl'k̲émtsin (Lytton). He attended St George's Indian Residential School for a short time, then ranched at 9 Mile, north of Tl'k̲émtsin. He had many head of cattle. Louie was a great hunter and knew every mountain in the area both by name and by location. He was also a great storyteller. When someone needed to know something about Tl'k̲émtsin or about Nlha7kápmx country, we'd say, 'Ask Louie Phillips.' Louie lived his life to the fullest.

Bert Seymour

Bert (b. 1931) is from Sxáxen̓x (Shackan) and is a member of the Shackan Indian Band. He has been a railway worker and a logger, and he has ranched at Sxáxen̓x for many years. He and his wife, Joyce, have four boys and four girls. They enjoy attending gatherings and pow-wows. Bert is active in furthering our language and culture. He has been a band councillor for twenty-seven years.

Rosie Skuki

Rosie (1880-1974) was born and raised in Tl'k̲émtsin (Lytton), where she also raised her own family. She was a member of the Lytton First Nation and she was a cedar-root basketmaker. She harvested all the materials for her baskets. Rosie obtained cedar-root baskets made by other women in exchange for second-hand clothing. She then resold these baskets (along with her own) as well as second-hand clothing in her own store in Tl'k̲émtsin. This store is still standing.

Nathan Spinks

Nathan (b. 1930) was born and raised in Tl'k̲émtsin (Lytton), where he worked on the railway. He and his wife, Rhoda, moved to Everett, Washington, so his children could get a good education. There, he worked as a log-scaler. They returned to Tl'k̲émtsin after their children finished school. Nathan is a former chief of the Lytton First Nation and is now a councillor. He is particularly interested in how fisheries and education matters affect the Nlha7kápmx people.

Dorothy Ursaki, translator

Dorothy (b. 1907) is from K'k̲émtsin (Spences Bridge). She attended the All Hallows School for Girls in Yale until she was ten. When that school was closed, she attended St George's Indian Residential School in Tl'k̲émtsin (Lytton) until she was fifteen. After finishing school, she returned to K'k̲émtsin and met her husband, Charles Ursaki. They raised their two children in Chilliwack. For the past twenty years, she has been busy researching our language, and she has compiled her own dictionary as well as archival records on Nlha7kápmx history in the K'k̲émtsin area. Today, she works with the Department of Linguistics at the University of British Columbia, assisting in field methods courses and helping students who are working on their Master's degrees.

BILL WALKEM

Bill (b. 1913), a brother of Dorothy Ursaki, attended St George's Indian Residential School and has lived in K'k̲émtsin (Spences Bridge) all his life. He mined and fished before working for the CNR, where he was a section and extra gang foreman until he retired. Today, he likes to read and reminisce about old times; he also enjoys gardening. Through Bill's knowledge, the Nkwi7tsútn celebration, which had not been held for over 100 years, was revitalized in 1993.

MARY WILLIAMS

Mary (Míli) (1898-1986) was born and raised at Mayxmtm (Snake Flat), near Tl'k̲émtsin (Lytton). She married Peter Charlie and had many children. Peter died shortly after Rita, their youngest child, was born. Míli later married Justice Williams and lived with him at Nx̲wúmin (near Earlscourt). They had one boy. Before she died, Míli lived with her daughter, Rita, in Tl'k̲émtsin. She was everyone's yáya7 (grandmother).

ANNIE YORK

Annie (1904-1991), one of seven brothers and sisters, was born at Spuzzum. She was educated at Pitt Meadows and moved to Merritt in 1925. While in Merritt she was a home nurse before becoming involved in interpreting for Nlha7kápmx people in the courts and hospitals. She moved back to Spuzzum in 1932. In the later part of her life, she worked with Laurence and Terry Thompson to develop a dictionary of our language. Her work with researchers has concluded with the publication of several invaluable books and papers on our language, traditions, and plant use. She was also featured in a film entitled *Bowl of Bone*. Annie was a friend to many people and never turned anyone away from her door.

Afterword

WE FIRST HEARD about Darwin Hanna's project from our elders, who were working with him to record the stories included in this book. We were familiar with the effort and dedication that Darwin had put into past projects, so we were confident that the stories would be recorded properly and that the elders would be treated with respect.

As a band council, we did not hesitate to recommend that our membership support this project; band members were equally excited and endorsed our recommendation. The most important qualities of our culture are our language and our stories. In oral traditions such as ours, telling stories is how we pass on the history and teachings of our ancestors. Without these stories, we would have to rely on other people for guidance and information about our past. Teachings in the form of stories are an integral part of our identity as a people and as a nation. If we lose these stories, we will do a disservice to our ancestors – those who gave us the responsibility to keep our culture alive.

In this age of instant communication through fax machines, telephones, television, and satellites, it is paradoxical that at no time in our history have we, as a people, been less close to each other. We are so busy working, raising families, and 'communicating' that we have forgotten how to speak and, more important, how to listen to one another. We don't get together unless it is for bingo, political meetings, funerals, or weddings – but at these meetings the pace is so fast that we rarely make time to listen to our elders and hear the stories. The old stories could take what is now considered a long time to tell – but in their telling we learn about each other and about our spirituality. In other words, we learn about what it means to be Nlha7kápmx. Today, if we cannot say things in thirty seconds, the younger generation finds it hard to sit and listen to us.

The effects of *not* making time to learn to tell the stories in the right way is now manifesting itself at the political level – chiefs and councillors who may not know each other, or who do not have a common base of experience and knowledge, tend to bicker over petty issues and, generally, do not develop respect for one another. The fast pace demanded by the outside world also makes it difficult for leaders to explain issues in a way that enables band members to make informed decisions. Some leaders offer their people only simple choices with respect to very complex issues – thus, in effect, making their decisions for them.

Our Tellings has come along at a critical time in our history. There are still elders who can remember and tell the stories, so it is important to record them. Unfortunately, more of these elders are dying each year, and with each death we lose another link to our past. The Cook's Ferry Band members resurrected an old meeting place, Nk̲w'i7tsútn, 'A Place to Dance.' This place is significant, because it was where Nlha7kápmx and our neighbours gathered in the month of August in order to hunt and gather food in the Twaal Valley area. It was also a time when people got together to socialize and when stories would be passed on to the new generation. For the initial gathering in 1993, Lillooet, Shuswap, and Okanagan peoples were invited to attend. These peoples came and shared with us their songs, dances, and stories, and they helped make the gathering a success.

The Nk̲w'i7tsútn gathering brought together over 300 people to a site that had not been used for this purpose for more than a hundred years. For everyone, it was a powerful, positive experience with strong spiritual overtones. For instance, according to the stories, there was a tree there that was a Grizzly dancing tree. Grizzly would dance in a circle around the tree, pushing up the earth and making a circle for the people to follow him. He would then leave his mark on the tree to let everyone know that this was his place and that it was a dancing spot. When we gathered in 1993, we were trying to learn and follow our customs as closely as we could; but, given that we had not done so in one hundred years, we could not do it perfectly.

After the opening ceremonies were finished, everyone began to listen to the tellers. At this time, storm clouds rolled up the valley and over the gathering, cutting out the sun and darkening the afternoon. A bolt of lightning lit up the north end of the valley, quickly followed by a second bolt, which lit up the south end of the valley. With a crash of thunder the heavens opened up, and it began to pour – soaking everyone. Later that evening, Bert Seymour, a Shackan elder and councillor who was the master of ceremonies, related to us that we had neglected to pay our respects to the spirit of Grizzly; thus, through the lightning, Grizzly was asking who was using his tree after such a long time. Grizzly then brought the rain to cleanse both the site and us – once he realized why we were there. Following Bert's advice, at the base of the tree we made an offering of tobacco to Grizzly. The rain then eased off, and the second day of celebration was mostly clear.

An equally powerful message was sent to those gathered on the final day. Thirty hand-drummers were completing their songs and ceremonies around the tree when two deer entered the north end of the field and bounded towards the sweathouse. After turning to look at the gathered drummers and dancers, the deer leisurely loped to the far end of the field and disappeared from view. This was interpreted to mean that the spirits of our ancestors were happy with what was happening – the rebirth and reaffirmation of our culture. It is at this type of gathering that the stories within this book must be told and retold as they are passed along to the next generation of storytellers.

There are no words to describe the gratitude we feel to our elders who worked so hard on this publication, contributing stories, translations, and encouragement. As in the past, our elders continue to show us leadership.

One key for us in making our decision to support this collection of stories is the character of Darwin Hanna. This work is just one example of the strength and dedication he brings to his work. We trust that each person who reads these stories will be touched in some way and will make it his or her responsibility to ensure that Nlha7kápmx culture does not die.

Chief David Walkem
Councillor M. Rose Spence
Councillor Jean York
Councillor Pearl Hewitt
Cook's Ferry Band Council

Appendix 1: Orthographic Key for the Nlha7kápmx Alphabet, Lytton Dialect

This is a key to the practical writing system used to transcribe the Nlha7kápmx words appearing in this book. The writing system used here is phonemic and was designed and put into use by Randy Bouchard and Mamie Henry in the early 1970s. Louie Phillips always checked their work.

There are 45 meaningful sound differences that must be expressed in writing the Nlha7kápmx language. Of the 26 symbols available in English, we use only 18, plus the symbol for the number seven (7). The remaining symbols for the Nlha7kápmx alphabet are obtained by using three special markings (an acute, an apostrophe, or an underline), along with the English alphabet symbols.

(1) A glottal stop is written as the number 7.

(2) The accent ´ written over a vowel indicates that the latter receives primary stress in all words containing two or more vowels.
á é í ó ú

(3) An apostrophe written following a consonant indicates a glottalized or 'strongly exploded' sound, while an apostrophe written above a consonant indicates a glottalized resonant or 'weakly exploded' sound.
strongly exploded: k' k̲' kw' k̲w' p' tl' ts'
weakly exploded: g̲̓ g̲̓w l' m̓ n̓ w̓ y̓ z̓

(4) The underlining of a consonant indicates uvulars and pharyngeals – sounds produced far back in the throat.
g̲ g̲w k̲ k̲' k̲w k̲w' x̲ x̲w

(5) A 'w' written beside a consonant indicates a labialized sound, produced with rounded lips.
g̲w kw kw' k̲w k̲w' xw x̲w

(6) Five phonemically distinct vowels are recognized and written as a, e, i, o, u. The orthographic symbols representing vowels are as follows:

a The Nlha7kápmx vowel sound represented by the alphabet symbol *a* is most often pronounced like the vowel sound in *bat*, but other related vowel sounds also represented by *a* may vary from a sound similar to that found in *bet* to a sound similar to that found in the first syllable of *father*.

e The Nlha7kápmx vowel sound represented by the alphabet symbol *e* is most often pronounced like the vowel sound in *earth*, but other related vowel sounds also represented by *e* may vary from a sound similar to that found in *but* to a sound similar to that found in *put*.

i The Nlha7kápmx sound represented by the alphabet symbol *i* is most often pronounced like the vowel sound in *beat*, but other related vowel sounds also represented by *i* may vary from a sound similar to that found in *bait* to a sound similar to that found in *bit*.

o The Nlha7kápmx vowel sound represented by the alphabet symbol *o* is most often pronounced like the vowel sound in English *bought*. Note that *o* occurs rarely in the Nlha7kápmx language.

u The Nlha7kápmx vowel sound represented by the alphabet symbol *u* is most often pronounced like the vowel sound in English *boot*, but other related vowel sounds also represented by *u* may vary from a sound similar to that found in *boat* to a sound similar to that found in *lord*.

(7) Symbols used to represent Nlha7kápmx sounds in approximately the same way that they represent corresponding English sounds are:
h k l m p s ss t ts w y z

(8) Symbols for special sounds which occur only in Nlha7kápmx, and for which there are no corresponding English alphabet symbols, are:
g lh x

Appendix 2: Key to Tapings, Translations, and Transcriptions

Individuals hold copyright to their own stories. Overall copyright on the work is held in trust by Synk'y'peplxw (Coyote House) Language and Culture Society and Mamie Henry.

Sptákwelh

'Ntl'ík'semtm (Coyote's Son),' told by Mildred Michell. Taped by Darwin Hanna and Mamie Henry in 1992, translated by Mamie Henry, transcribed by Darwin Hanna.

'Coyote and His Son,' told by Walter Isaac. Taped by Randy Bouchard in 1968, translated by Mamie Henry, transcribed by the British Columbia Indian Language project (BCILP).

'The Trip to the Moon,' told by Annie York. Taped and translated by Mamie Henry in 1973, transcribed by BCILP.

'Coyote and the Three Sisters,' told by Louie Phillips. Taped by Darwin Hanna in 1992, transcribed by Darwin Hanna.

'Coyote and Wolf,' told by Herb Manuel. Taped by Darwin Hanna in 1992, transcribed by Darwin Hanna.

'Coyote and Buffalo,' told by Herb Manuel. Taped by Darwin Hanna in 1992, transcribed by Darwin Hanna.

'Coyote and Wood Tick,' told by Herb Manuel. Taped by Darwin Hanna in 1992, transcribed by Darwin Hanna.

'Coyote Visits His Daughter in the North,' told by Herb Manuel. Taped by Darwin Hanna in 1992, transcribed by Darwin Hanna.

'Coyote and the Two Sisters,' told by Mandy Brown. Taped by Darwin Hanna in 1992, transcribed by Darwin Hanna.

'Why Newborn Animals Can Walk,' told by Mandy Brown. Taped by Darwin Hanna in 1992, transcribed by Darwin Hanna.

'Grizzly and the Bear Cubs,' told by Hilda Austin. Taped by Darwin Hanna and Mamie Henry in 1992, translated by Dorothy Ursaki, transcribed by Darwin Hanna.

'Grizzly and the Black Bear Cubs,' told by Mary Williams, Taped by Mamie Henry and Tammy Hurst in 1971, translated by Mamie Henry, transcribed by BCILP.

'The Four Bear Brothers,' told by Anthony Joe. Taped by Mamie Henry and Tammy Hurst in 1971, translated by Mamie Henry, transcribed by BCILP.

'Transformers,' told by Louie Phillips. Taped by Darwin Hanna in 1992, transcribed by Darwin Hanna.

'Transformers,' told by Herb Manuel. Taped by Darwin Hanna in 1992, transcribed by Darwin Hanna.

'Transformer Footprints,' told by Louie Phillips. Taped by Darwin Hanna in 1992, transcribed by Darwin Hanna.

'How Chipmunk Got His Stripes,' told by Mandy Brown. Taped by Darwin Hanna in 1992, transcribed by Darwin Hanna.

'Screech Owl,' told by Mandy Brown. Told to Darwin Hanna in 1992, translated by Dorothy Ursaki, transcribed by Darwin Hanna.

'Raven,' told by Mandy Brown. Told to Darwin Hanna in 1992, translated by Dorothy Ursaki, transcribed by Darwin Hanna.

'The Boy Who Was Abandoned,' told by Mary Williams. Taped by Mamie Henry and Tammy Hurst in 1971, translated by Mamie Henry, transcribed by BCILP.

'Sore Man,' told by Mabel Joe. Taped by Darwin Hanna in 1992, translated by Dorothy Ursaki, transcribed by Darwin Hanna.

'Man and Owl,' told by Mabel Joe. Taped by Darwin Hanna in 1992, translated by Dorothy Ursaki, transcribed by Darwin Hanna.

'Dog Travels to the Sun,' told by Mabel Joe. Taped by Darwin Hanna in 1992, translated by Dorothy Ursaki, transcribed by Darwin Hanna.

'The Country Divided,' told by Annie York. Taped by Mamie Henry in 1973, translated by Mamie Henry, transcribed by BCILP.

'Grandfather and Grandson Work for Gold and Silver,' told by Tom George. Taped by Darwin Hanna and Jack Joe in 1992, translated by Dorothy Ursaki, transcribed by Darwin Hanna.

Spílaxem

'The Lost Hunter,' told by Mabel Joe. Taped by Darwin Hanna in 1992, translated by Dorothy Ursaki, transcribed by Darwin Hanna.

'Smuy̓mn (Person with a Cane),' told by Peter Bob. Taped by Darwin Hanna in 1992, translated by Bert Seymour, transcribed by Darwin Hanna.

'Why There Are Nlha7kápmx in Spokane,' told by Mabel Joe. Taped by Darwin Hanna and Mamie Henry in 1992, translated by Dorothy Ursaki, transcribed by Darwin Hanna.

'Sexpínlhemx's Wife Foretells the Coming of the White Man,' told by Annie York. Taped by Imbert Orchard in 1965, transcribed by Darwin Hanna.

'Simon Fraser,' told by Annie York. Taped by Imbert Orchard in 1965, transcribed by Darwin Hanna.

'First Encounter with Missionaries,' told by Annie York. Taped by Imbert Orchard in 1965, transcribed by Darwin Hanna.

'The Coming of the White Man,' told by Mary Williams. Taped by Mamie Henry and Tammy Hurst in 1971, translated by Mamie Henry, transcribed by BCILP.

'Sun Dance,' written by Bill Walkem in 1993.

'Nk̲w'i7tsútn (A Place to Dance),' told by Bill Walkem. Taped by Darwin Hanna in 1993, transcribed by Darwin Hanna.

'Archdeacon Small,' told by Bill Walkem. Taped by Darwin Hanna in 1993, transcribed by Darwin Hanna.

'Xítl'ix (Nlha7kápmx Court),' told by Louie Phillips. Taped by Darwin Hanna in 1991, transcribed by Darwin Hanna.

'Old Ways,' written by Nathan Spinks in 1991.

'Power of the Sexwná7m (Healer/Doctor),' told by Tom George and Bert Seymour. Taped by Darwin Hanna, translated by Marion Bent, transcribed by Darwin Hanna.

'On the Boston Bar Trail,' told by Peter Bob. Taped by Darwin Hanna in 1992, transcribed by Darwin Hanna.

'Listening to Stories,' told by Peter Bob. Taped by Darwin Hanna in 1992, transcribed by Darwin Hanna.

'On the Trapline,' told by Phil Acar. Taped by Darwin Hanna and Mamie Henry, transcribed by Darwin Hanna.

'Our Tellings,' told by Louie Phillips. Taped by Darwin Hanna in 1992, transcribed by Darwin Hanna.

'Making Baskets,' told by Rosie Skuki. Taped by Mamie Henry and Tammy Hurst in 1971, translated by Mamie Henry, transcribed by BCILP.

'Native Foods,' told by Christine Bobb. Taped by Mamie Henry and Tammy Hurst in 1971, translated by Mamie Henry, transcribed by BCILP.

'Trips to Petáni,' told by Mary Williams. Taped and translated by Mamie Henry in 1973, transcribed by BCILP.

'The Road to Petáni Valley,' told by Mary Williams. Taped and translated by Mamie Henry in 1973, transcribed by BCILP.

'Ways of the Old People,' told by Mandy Brown. Taped by Darwin Hanna in 1992, transcribed by Darwin Hanna.

'Memories of Lytton,' told by Edna Malloway. Taped by Darwin Hanna in 1992, transcribed by Darwin Hanna.

'Passing on the Knowledge,' told by Fred, Bea, and Buddy Hanna. Taped by Darwin Hanna in 1992, transcribed by Darwin Hanna.

Glossary of Nlha7kápmx Words

ha7í. Yes.

hátsu. Let’s go.

hi7. Wailing sound.

imts. Grandson.

k̲álex̲. Digging stick.

k’ám̓a. Pine needles.

K’ásu. Personal name.

Kelhtatálhen̓k̲wa7. Name of one of Coyote’s sons.

K’k̲émtsin. Spences Bridge.

K̲wék̲etl’t. Always Smiling (name of young bear cub).

kwesp. Buffalo (Okanagan language).

k̲wtíx̲a7. Louse.

k̲wúm̓xen. Chipmunk.

kw’úna. Aged salmon eggs.

Kw’úwa7. Personal name.

Lamín̓ak. Personal name.

lhkw̓úsa7ma. Game that involves throwing an object into the air and piercing it with a dart.

máwits. Deer (Chinook trade language).

Mím̓li. Mildred Michell’s name.

mula7. Edible bulb.

Nek̲’na7k̲’í7x. Name of a place on the way to Petáni where a few of the trees are twisted back.

Ngwúyuym̓xw. Place-name.

Nk̲’awmn. Nicomen/Thompson Siding.

Nk̲á7ya. Niakia.

Nk’iyápaplhxw. Name of one of Coyote’s sons.

Nkwelkwelhí7t. Mountain berries.

Nk̲wi7íkn̓. 9 Mile, north of Lytton.

N<u>k</u>w'i7tsútn. A Place to Dance.

Nlha7kápmx. The Nlha7kápmx nation and people of south-central British Columbia.

Nlha7kapmxtsín. The Nlha7kápmx language.

nmitsa7<u>k</u>wúps. To ride behind a person on a saddle.

Npa7tsítsi7t. Little bear.

Npatús. Narrow valley on the north side of the Stein River.

Npuypíychen. Place-name, north of Lytton.

Ntl'ík'semtm. Name of one of Coyote's sons.

ntuw̓. Sap.

nú<u>x</u>wa. Sweetheart.

N<u>x</u>awléts. Personal name.

n<u>x</u>a7<u>x</u>a7átkwu. Powerful, spooky, scary place.

N<u>x</u>wu7mín. Nohomeen.

Pálak. Personal name.

Petáni Valley. Botanie Valley.

P'<u>k</u>aý̓st. Mile 89.

S7áa7. Crow (Louie Phillips' name).

sáma7. White person or people.

S7ámteka. Personal name.

Sáplow. Personal name.

Senk'iy̓áp. Coyote.

Senk'iy̓apáplhxw. Coyote's House.

Sexpínlhemx. Head Chief David Spintlum.

sexwná7m. Healer/doctor.

s7istkn. Pithouse (semi-subterranean winter home), also referred to as a kwickwillie house.

Síswa7. Name of Coyote's youngest son.

skalúla7. Owl.

sk'ám̓ats. Root of the yellow avalanche lily.

S<u>k</u>waní7<u>k</u>wa. Grandfather of Four Bear Brothers.

Skweláltkwu. Name of a spring.

Skwikwtl'kwetl't. Female Bear's youngest cub.

slahal. Bone game; gambling game.

smuy̓mn. Person with a cane.

spá7ats. Bear.

Spápiyem̓. Place-name.

Sp'áp'ts'en̓. Spatsum.

sp'áts'en. Hemp.

spílaxem. Non-creation stories, relating to events that occurred during historical time.

sptákwelh. Creation stories, relating to events that occurred when the world was populated by animals in human form.

Stemálst. Personal name.

stsákwem. Saskatoon berry.

sts'uwén. Dried salmon.

sts'wenay̓tmx. Sasquatch.

Sulús. Shulus.

suxwsúxw. Grizzly.

swáwem. Gathering.

Sxáxen̓x. Shackan/14 Mile.

Sxáysemkn. Personal name.

sxwe7úlh. Awl.

Sxwitl'áts'ank. Mountain goat.

sxwúsem. Soapberry.

tatúwen̓. Corms of the western spring beauty, also known as wild potatoes.

Telhníts'a7. John Tetlinitsa.

Tl'kémtsin. The Village of Lytton, at the confluence of the Fraser and Thompson rivers.

tl'úxwen̓. Horsetail plant.

Tsawtemxínak. Personal name.

ts'ek7áwlh. Canoe.

Ts’ek̲7awlhák̲s. Place-name for piece of land shaped like a canoe.

Tselhnéga n skwast. My name is Tselhnéga.

ts’ets’ék̲w’. Markings made from red ochre.

ts’itl’. Pitch.

tsúg̲wlha7. Steelhead.

Tsukw tl’u7 a np’u7tns. Only his behind.

Tsukw tl’u7 a sk’emálhxwi7ts. Only his Adam’s apple.

Tu. Sound.

wiy̓e. Black tree lichen; Spanish moss.

Wísiyem̓xw. High Mountain (place-name).

x̲a7x̲á7. Powerful, sacred.

xítl’ix. To kneel; Nlha7kápmx court.

yámit. Prayer.

yáya7. Grandmother.

Yi7áneknlháwstn. Name of one of Coyote’s sons.

yi7áy. Yes, when encouraging tellers to continue talking.

Yúg̲̓la7. Paul Yoala.

Zexzéx. Mudslide (place-name).

zíxa. Down.

Bibliography

Bouchard, Randy, and Dorothy Kennedy. 1988. 'Indian Land Use and Indian History of the Stein River Valley, British Columbia.' Report prepared for I.R. Wilson Consultants Ltd. and British Columbia Forest Products Ltd.

Drake-Terry, Joanne. 1989. *The Same as Yesterday: The Lillooet Chronicle the Theft of Their Lands and Resources.* Lillooet: Lillooet Tribal Council

Egesdal, Steven M. 1992. *Stylized Characters' Speech in Thompson Salish Narrative. University of Montana Occasional Papers in Linguistics* no. 9. Missoula, MT: University of Montana Linguistics Laboratory

Gioe, Heister Dean, ed. 1990. *Coyote Stories by Mourning Dove.* Notes by L.V. McWhorter (Old Wolf). Introduction and notes to the Bison Book Edition written by Jay Miller. Lincoln: University of Nebraska Press

Hanna, Darwin. 1994. 'Justice the Nlha7kápmx Way.' Unpublished paper

Harris, Cole. 1992. 'The Fraser River Canyon Encountered.' *BC Studies* 94:5-28

Henry, Mamie, and Randy Bouchard. 1974. 'Lytton Thompson Language Dialect.' Unpublished paper

Kirkness, Verna. 1994. *Khot-La-Cha: The Autobiography of Chief Simon Baker.* Douglas & McIntyre

Laforet, Andrea. 1987. 'The Nlaka'pamux People: A Brief Sketch.' Unpublished paper. Ottawa: Canadian Museum of Civilization

Laforet, Andrea, and Annie York. 1981. 'Notes on the Thompson Winter Dwelling.' In *The World is as Sharp as a Knife: An Anthology in Honour of Wilson Duff*, edited by Donald N. Abbott, 115-22. Victoria: British Columbia Provincial Museum

Laforet, Andrea, Nancy J. Turner, and Annie York. 1993. 'Traditional Foods of the Fraser Canyon Nlaka'pamux.' In *American Indian Linguistics and Ethnography in Honor of Laurence C. Thompson*, edited by Anthony Mattina and Timothy Montler, 191-213. *University of Montana Occasional Papers in Linguistics* no. 10. Missoula, MT: University of Montana Linguistics Laboratory

Lamb, Kaye, W. 1960. *The Letters and Journals of Simon Fraser 1806-1808.* Toronto: Macmillan

Lean, Pat. 1979. 'Commemorating: James Alexander Teit.' *Nicola Valley Historical Quarterly* 2 (2):1-8

M'Gonigle, Michael, and Wendy Wickwire. 1988. *Stein: The Way of the River*. Vancouver: Talonbooks

Maud, Ralph, ed. 1978. *The Salish People: The Local Contribution of Charles Hill-Tout*. Vol. 1, *The Thompson and the Okanagan*. Vancouver: Talonbooks

—. 1982. *A Guide to BC Indian Myth and Legend*. Vancouver: Talonbooks

Meggs, Geoff. 1989. 'Blockade at Hell's Gate.' *Fisherman* 54 (12):24

Mohs, Gordon. 1986. 'Alliance Oral History: Nlaka'pamux Transcripts/Summaries of Taped Interviews with Elders.' On file at Nlaka'pamux Nation Tribal Council

Muller, Haike, and Shirley Sterling, eds. 1994. *My Family, My Strength: A Collection of Illustrated Stories by First Nations Children across British Columbia*. Vancouver: Native Indian Teacher Education Program

Robinson, Harry, and Wendy Wickwire. 1989. *Write It on Your Heart: The Epic World of an Okanagan Storyteller*. Vancouver: Talonbooks/Theytus

Sproat, G. 1979. 'Report to Superintendent General of Indian Affairs on Resolutions of Nl'akapxm Meeting, July 1879.' Black Series, National Archives of Canada, RG 10, vol. 3696, file 15,316

Steltzer, Uli. 1976. *Indian Artists at Work*. Vancouver: Douglas & McIntyre

Sterling, Shirley. 1992. *My Name Is Seepeetza*. Vancouver: Douglas & McIntyre

Stewart, Noel. (n.d.). *'Meet Mr Coyote': A Series of BC Indian Legends (Thompson Tribe)*. Victoria: Victoria Branch of the Society for the Furtherance of BC Tribal Arts and Crafts

Teit, James. 1898. *Traditions of the Thompson River Indians of British Columbia*. New York: Houghton-Mifflin

—. 1900. 'The Thompson Indians of British Columbia.' *Memoirs of the American Museum of Natural History* 2:163-392

—. 1912. 'Mythology of the Thompson Indians.' *Memoirs of the American Museum of Natural History* 12:199-416

—. 1916. 'European Tales from the Upper Thompson Indians.' *Journal of American Folklore* 29 (113):301-29

—. 1917. 'Thompson Tales.' *Memoirs of the American Folklore Society* 11:1-64

—. 1937. 'More Thompson Tales.' *Journal of American Folklore* 50 (196):173-90

Thompson, Laurence C., and M. Terry Thompson. In press. *A Dictionary of Thompson River Salish, with English Finder List. University of Montana Occasional Papers in Linguistics* no. 11. Missoula, MT: University of Montana Linguistics Laboratory

Thompson, Terry, and Steven M. Egesdal. 1993. 'Annie York's Push-Back-Sides-of-His-Hair: A Traditional Thompson River Salish Legend with Commentary.' In *American Indian Linguistics and Ethnography in Honor of Laurence C. Thompson*, edited by Anthony Mattina and Timothy Montler, 279-302. *University of Montana Occasional Papers in Linguistics* no. 10. Missoula, MT: University of Montana Linguistics Laboratory

Turner, Nancy J., Laurence C. Thompson, M. Terry Tompson, and Annie Z. York. 1990. *Thompson Ethnobotany. Royal British Columbia Museum Memoir* 3. Victoria: Royal British Columbia Museum

Wickwire, Wendy. 1991. 'Anthropology and Native Resistance in South Central British Columbia, 1908-1922.' Unpublished paper

—. 1993. 'Women in Ethnography: The Research of James Teit.' *Ethnohistory* 40 (4):539-62

—. 1994. 'To See Ourselves As the Other's Other: Nlaka'pamux Contact Narratives.' *Canadian Historical Review* 75 (1):1-20

York, Annie, Richard Daly, and Chris Arnett. 1993. *They Write Their Dreams on the Rock Forever: Rock Writings in the Stein River Valley of British Columbia*. Vancouver: Talonbooks

Set in Quadraat
Text design: George Vaitkunas
Printed and bound in Canada by Friesens
Copy-editor: Joanne Richardson
Proofreader: Camilla Jenkins
Cartographer: Eric Leinberger

1005582471